AF531390

INDIA BOOKVARSITY

LOTUS CHOICES

Editor: Mahendra Kulasrestha

The Discourses of Lord Buddha

The Wonderful Sutta Nipata

Translated by V. Fausball

The Ramayana of Buddhism

Drawings based on
Ajanta Paintings by
Reliable Infomedia

4263/3, Ansari Road,
Darya Ganj, New Delhi- 110002

THE DISCOURSES OF LORD BUDDHA

A Canonical Text of Buddhism-Sutta Nipata
Translated from the Pali
by V. Fausball

Source: Sutta Nipata, Translated by V. Fausball, Sacred Books of the East, Vol. 10, Oxford University Press, 1894.

The Discourses of Lord Buddha

First Edition—2010

ISBN: 978-81-8382-202-2 (H/B)

Published by:
Lotus Press
4263/3, Ansari Road, Darya Ganj,
New Delhi-10002
Ph.: 32903912, 23280047
E-mail: lotus_press@sify.com
www.lotuspress.co.in

Laser Typeset by: **Upasana Graphics**, Delhi

Printed at: **Anand Sons, Delhi**

Buddham Sharnam

Buddha, the Marvellous

–Vivekananda

Buddhism is historically the most important religion because it was the most tremendous movement the world ever saw, the most gigantic spiritual wave ever to burst upon human society. **There is no civilisation on which its effect has not been felt in some way or the other.**

The followers of Buddha were most enthusiastic and very missionary in spirit. They were the first not to remain content with the limited sphere of their mother church. They travelled east and west, north and south. They went into Persia, Asia Minor, Russia, Poland,...China, Korea, Japan,.. Burma, Siam and beyond.

The civilisation of India has died and revived several times. This is its peculiarity. At the time Buddha was born, India was in need of a great spiritual leader. There was a most powerful body of priests... The Brahmins began to arrogate powers and privileges to themselves. If a Brahmin killed a man, he would not be punished, even the most wicked Brahmin must be worshipped....two thousand ceremonies they had invented. India was full of it in Buddha's day.

At last one man could bear it no more. He had the brain, the power and the heart—a heart as infinite as the broad sky. He learnt why men suffer, and he found the way out of suffering. **Buddha was the first great preacher of equality.** Every man and woman had the same right to attain spirituality, he opened the door of Nirvana to one and all, even the lowest were entitled to highest attainment. His teaching was bold even for India.

The religion of Buddha spread fast. It was because of the marvellous love which, for the first time in the history of humanity, devoted itself to the service not only of all men but of all living things.

Buddha's idea is that **there is no God, only man himself.** He repudiated the mentality which underlies the prevalent ideas of God. He found it made men weak and superstitious. Everything independent is happy, everything dependent is miserable.

All my life I've been very fond of Buddha. I've more veneration for that character than for any other – that boldness, that fearlessness, and that tremendous love! He was born for the good of men. He sought truth because people were in misery – how to help them, was his only concern.

And consider his marvellous brain! Believe not because an old manuscript says so, but think for yourself, search truth for yourself, realise it yourself — then if you find it beneficial, give it to people.

And consider his death. He ate food offered to him by an outcast, a *chandal.* He told his disciples not to eat this food; 'but I cannot refuse it; go to the man and tell him he has done me one of the greatest services of my life; he has released me from this body.'

His method of work and organisation was quite striking. The idea that we have today of Church is his creation. He organised the monks and made them into a body. Even the voting by ballot is there, 560 years before Christ. **It was the foundation of Christian religion**; the Catholic Church came from Buddhism.

He was the only man who was even ready to give up his life for animals to stop a sacrifice. He once said to a king, 'If the sacrifice of a lamb helps you to go to heaven, sacrificing a man will help you better. So sacrifice me.' This man set in motion the highest moral ideas any people can have.

To many the path becomes easier if they believe in God. But the life of Buddha shows that even a man who does not believe in God, has no metaphysics, belongs to no sect and goes not to any church, or temple, and is a confessed materialist, even he can attain to the highest.

Editorspeak

THE SECOND SPREAD

It would seem that the seeds of a second spread of Buddhism in the world have been sown, awaiting the growing up of the trees, their flowering and fruition. As the present writer was preparing to pen down this note, the ever enchanting (though in political matters not so attractive) 'Outlook' weekly published a long article entitled 'Return of the Buddha', essentially reporting the opening ceremony of the Rs. 100 crore Vipassana Pagoda in an island close to Mumbai, Gorai, the largest dome in the world, attended by The President of India, a large number of celebrities, among whom was 'Buddha's star new-age disciple', Priyanka Gandhi Vadra. It was news to me as I didn't find it in my daily newspaper, The Hindustan Times. The quite thorough presenter Sheela Reddy related the story in a wider perspective, highlighting other similar movements, including the Soka Gakkai of the Japanese preacher Daisaku Ikeda, which is now 'flourishing into tens of millions.'

Since I was also involved over a decade ago in one similar effort inspired by a Japanese nun, a disciple of the famous Fuji Guruji, the monk who gave the three monkeys to Mahatma Gandhi; but most unfortunately, the great effort did not materialise — and I still wonder why the invisible Buddha spirits in heavens did not support it. The whole story in described in the Gandhi Album published by me in those days, a copy of which when I presented it to the former Prime Minister P.V. Narsimha Rao in later years—when I had the facility of meeting him while publishing the Hindi version of his delightfully well written political novel 'The Insider,'—cheerfully enquired why the project was not carried out, I unhesitatingly told him, 'You were the Prime Minister, Sir, at that time, and your office did not respond, *despite the fact that I had got a letter written to you by the then President of India, the soft-spoken Dr. Shankar Dayal Sharma himself,* who was quite happy at the project being carried out in the capital of the country, at Gandhi Samadhi itself, because he had inaugurated a few months ago a similar Peace Pagoda in Wardha. ('The former P.M. pouted a little as was his wont and kept quiet. I also asked him to read the last four pages of the Album, which also states that *Pt. Nehru himself had initiated a pagoda at Rajgir when he was Prime Minister,* but could not carry it out... He pouted a little more but did not utter a word.... I've a few more tales regarding my talks with him, some quite good, but this is perhaps no place to relate them.)

A sad story indeed, which started flowing from my Cello pen without my knowing it, and now I think it is alright because it does have historical value in the present context, and also because, I feel great angst at the Buddhistic Spirits — if they really exist — killing it most violently despite my/ our devotion and labour put in for it...

To return, 50 years ago, Buddhism opened its arms wide open to Dr. Ambedkar and his followers in an effort to compensate for the Untouchability Sin of its fellow religion despite the efforts of the great Sanatani Hindu Mahatma Gandhi, as well as the earliar Vivekananda—glory to it for this most wonderful historical act! It is now, according to the 'Outlook' report, '.....there is a new wave of Indians —affluent, national, metropolitan, English-educated individuals impatient of organised religion, are seeking in Buddhism the solutions to their myriad modern-day problems such as nuclear families, generation gap, divorces. collapse of family support systems, relationships, pressures of jobs and joblessness, lifestyle diseases, teenage angst and loneliness.' —Wow! sounds truly big and comprehensive. It would seem that the way things are moving –with Dalai Lama (whose story in India I'm presently tranlating into Hindi), Shantum Seth (the writer Vikram Seth's brother), the latest Vietnamese preacher Thich Nhat Hanh, and of course Satynarayan Goenka, to whom goes the total credit of promoting Vipassana in the country, who utilised his Marwari genius to collect the money also to build the pagoda – a kind of human revolution leading people to build up a new world on the basis of Gotama Buddha's 'core values of peace and non-violence' even managing the issues like global warming, nuclear danger and greening of the earth. The report concludes:'There is no way out for us except the Buddha's way.' Most heartening indeed!

So, Buddhism seems to serve both segments of society: the Dalit as well as the very rich; and the present writer would add, that it should take up another Indian senior, Rabindranath Tagore's advice: to 'mutate' our castes to complete the ancient Indian experiment — he finds it parallel to the American white-and-black problem of developing a total human society (I've highlighted this in my volume 'Tagore Select' published earlier in this series) which will be a great contribution to give a real human face to our society.

Buddhism has a background in Europe and America also. The study of the religion in the West dates back since the later years of the eighteenth century. In the nineteenth century large numbers of Chinese entered the country as labour on the construction of railroads, with whom came the religion. The Parliament of Religions in Chicago in 1893 was held – which threw up Vivekananda and made him famous worldwide – where several Buddhist sects were also represented and well received. Their teachers started visiting the country and within a few decades nearly all the schools of Buddhism opened their branches, and many Americans as well as Jews were converted. A few magazines were also started and conferences organised. The American Buddhist Congress held in 1987 suggested that there would be three to five million Buddhists in America, though it sounds exaggerated. There were over 50 thousand in Canada.

It England the Buddhist Society of Great Britain and Ireland was started in 1907, which published a magazine 'The Buddhist Review'. Later a Buddhist Lodge of the Theosophical Society was set up in 1924, which started the journal 'The Middle Way'. In 1967 a Friends of the Buddhist

Order was organised, which has been trying to give a Western shape to the religion. Among European countries Germany, France, Belgium, Holland, Italy, Switzerland, Norway and Sweden have groups interested in the religion. In the last decades of the century Fuji Guruji started a new movement of organising Peace Marches and establishing Peace Pagodas - of which the event told by me was a part - which in the initial stages was quite successful and effective but soon lost steam owing to a variety of reasons. Their Peace March across America was a grand event and their Peace Pagodas in many prominent cities, including London, did help create a powerful feeling in favour of Peace. As I had the opportunity to be associated with it, though at the margin, I can say that a lack of leadership — not of resources-, made further ineffective by their lack of facility in English - a common and close to insurmountable problem with the otherwise wonderful Japanese - was the cause of its fizzling out. In my view it had very solid potential, and can still be worked out— perhaps.

It is said that Buddhist groups are beginning to appear in South America, Africa and Australia also, and given their deep sympathy to the Tibetan cause, which expressed itself in their carefully planned outbursts during the Chinese Olympics, they seem to have stamina as well as the will to forcefully act. What is needed is broader planning, networking and action on a wider platform. A second Ashok is perhaps needed to make it serve its purpose and guide humanity on the right path.

•

This set of a few books on Lord Buddha and his religion has been planned with a view to provide middle-level literature for the common people: the first one presents a life of the Lord by the famous Asvaghosha, 'Buddha Charita', of the second century A.D., translated into English by E.B. Cowell, and this second one of the Lord's discourses, 'Sutta Nipata' (A Bunch of Discourses), translated by V. Fausball from the original in Pali, both of which taken together form a complete introduction to the subject. The third is intended to be the 'Mahaparinibbana Sutta', which provides further details of his life, which are moving in the extreme and complete the story of Buddha's eventful life. The fourth intended is 'Dhammapada', comparable in influence to the Gita of Hindu religions, though its subject-matter is different and may be described as a book of good behaviour and morals. The editor hopes that these works will be of use to those interested in Buddhism and be welcomed by them.

Buddham Sharanam.... Dhammam Sharanam...

Translatorspeak

THE BUDDHA AND HIS DHAMMA

The Collection of Discourses, 'Sutta-Nipata', which I have here translated, is very remarkable, as there can be no doubt that it contains some remnants of primitive Buddhism. I consider the greater part of the 'Mahavagga', and nearly the whole of the 'Atthakavagga' as very old. I have arrived at this conclusion from two reasons, first from the language, and secondly, from the contents.

We not only find here what we meet with in other Pali poetry, the fuller Vedic forms of nouns and verbs in the plural, the shorter Vedic plurals and the instrumental singular of nouns, Vedic infinitives, contracted (or sometimes old) forms, by the side of protracted forms, but also some unusual (sometimes old) forms and words. We also find nemesis as in the Vedas. Sometimes we meet with difficult and irregular constructions, and very condensed expressions. All this proves, I think, that these parts of the book are much older than the Suttas in which the language is not only fluent, but of which some verses are even singularly melodious.

In the contents we have an important contribution to the right understanding of primitive Buddhism, for we see here a picture not of life in monasteries, but of the life of hermits in its first stage. We have before us not the systematizing of the later Buddhist church, but the first germs of a system, the fundamental ideas of which come out with sufficient clearness.

Indian society at the time of Buddha had two large and distinguished religious sects, Samanas and Brahminas. This is apparent from several passages where they are mentioned together. Famous teachers arose and gathered around them flocks of disciples. As such are mentioned Purana-Kassapa,

Makkhali-Gosala, Ajita-Kesakambali, Pakudha-Nataputta; besides these there is Bavari and his disciples Ajita-Tissametteyya, Punnaka, Mettagu, Dhotaka, Upasiva, Nanda, Hemaka, Todeyya, Kappa, Jatukannin, Bhadravudha, Udaya, Posala, Mogharagan, Sela, Chankin, Tarukkha, Pokkhara-sati, Janussoni, Vasettha, and Bharadvaja.

We learn that there were four kinds of Samanas: Maggajinas, Maggadesakas, Maggajivins, and Maggadusins Among these Samanas disputes arose, a number of philosophical systems were formed, and at the time of Buddha there were as many as sixty-three of them. These systems are generally designated by *ditthi* or by *ditthasuta*, or by *dittha*, *suta*, and *muta*, or by *dittha*, *suta*, *silavata* and *muta*. The doctrines themselves are called *ditthinivesa*, or *nivesana*, or *vinichchaya*, and he who entertains any of them, is called *nivissavadin*.

What is said of the Samanas seems mostly to hold good about the Brahminas also. They too are called disputatious, *vadasila*, and three kinds of them are mentioned: Titthiyas, Ajivikas, and Niganthas. In contradistinction to the Samanas the Brahminas are designated as Tevijjas, they are Padakas, Veyyakaranas, and perfect in Jappa, Nighantu, Ketubha-Itihasa. They are called friends of the hymns, well versed in the hymns, and their principal hymn is Savitti. They worship and make offerings to the fire. In *Brahmanadhammika-sutta* the ancient and just Brahminas are described in opposition to the later Brahminas, who slay innocent cows and have acquired wealth through the favour of the kings.

All these disputants hold to their own prejudiced views. They say that purity comes from philosophical views, from tradition, and from virtuous works, and in many other ways, and that there is no bliss excepting by following their opinions.

Buddha himself has, it is true, sprung from the Samanas; he is called Samana Gotama, he shines like a sun in the midst of the Samanas, and intercourse with Samanas is said to be the highest blessing. But Buddha has overcome all their systems, there is nothing which has not been seen, heard, or thought by him and nothing which has not been understood by him. All the disputatious Brahminas do not overcome him in understanding and he asserts that no one is purified and saved by philosophy or by virtuous works. Sanctification, in fact, does not come from another, it can be attained only by going into the yoke with Buddha, by believing in him and in the Dhamma of the Saints, on the whole, by being what Buddha is.

What then is Buddha?

First he is a Visionary, in the good sense of the word; his knowledge is intuitive. 'Seeing misery,' he says, 'in the philosophical views, without adopting any of them, searching for truth, I saw inward peace.' And again: 'He, a conqueror unconquered, saw Dhamma visibly without any traditional instruction.' He teaches an instantaneous, an immediate religious life. He is called *chakkhumat*, endowed with an eye, clearly-seeing, *samantachakkhu*, the all-seeing, and as such he has become an eye to the world. He sees the subtle meaning of things, he is, in one word, Sambuddha, the perfectly-enlightened, and by knowledge he is delivered. Existence is *avijja*, ignorance, *vijja*, knowledge, is the extinction of the world.

Secondly, he is an Ascetic, a Muni, one that forsakes the world and wanders from the house to the houseless state, because from house-life arises defilement. Buddha is sometimes styled the great Isi, sometimes a Muni, sometimes a Brahmina, sometimes Bhikkhu, and all these appellations are used synonymously. Ascetic life is praised throughout the book. An ascetic has no prejudiced ideas, he has shaken off every philosophical view, he does not enter into disputes, he is not pleased nor displeased with a thing, he is indifferent to learning, he does not cling to good and evil, he has cut off all passion and all desire, he is free from marks, and possessionless, *akinchana*. He is equable, under all circumstances the same, still as the deep water, calm. He has reached peace, he knows that bliss consists in peace, he has gone to immortal peace, the unchangeable state of Nibbana. And how is this state brought about? By the destruction of consciousness. And how does consciousness cease? By the cessation of sensation.

What then is sin according to Buddha?

Subjectively, sin is desire, in all its various forms, desire for existence generally, and specially for name and form, i.e., individual existence. As long as man is led by desire he will be whirled about in existence, for as long as there is birth, there will be death. Existence is called the stream of death, the realm of Mara. Those who continually go to *samsara* with birth and death, are the ignorant.

But desire originates in the body, sin lies objectively in embodiment of matter, and consequently the human body is looked upon as a contemptible thing.

And what is bliss?

Subjectively, it is emancipation from desire by means of the peace that Buddha preaches.

Objectively, it is emancipation from body and matter. One must destroy the elements of existence, *upadhi*, and leave the body behind, that one may not come to exist again. The ignorant only create *upadhi*, and go again and again to *samsara*. The wise do not enter time, *kappa*, they look upon the world as void, hold that there is nothing really existing, and those whose minds are disgusted with a future existence, the wise who have destroyed their seeds of existence, go out like a lamp. As a flame blown about by the violence of the wind, goes out, and cannot be reckoned as existing, even so Muni, delivered from name and body, disappears, and cannot be reckoned as existing. For him who has disappeared, there is no form; that by which they say he is, exists for him no longer.

'Exert thyself, then—O Dhotaka,' so said Bhagavat, —'being wise and thoughtful in this world, let one, having listened to my utterance, learn his own extinction.'

With this short sketch of the contents of the 'Sutta Nipata' for a guide, I trust it will be easy to understand even the more obscure parts of the book.

Copenhagen, 1880.

Words the meaning of which is not always given in the translation

Ajivika, one belonging to a sect of naked ascetics.
Arahat, a holy man, a saint.
Ariya, Arya, noble.
Bhagavat, worshipful, blessed, a name of Buddha.
Bhikkhu, a mendicant.
Brahman, the supreme god of the Hindus.
Buddha, enlightened, a name of certain holy men who have freed themselves from existence, particularly of Samana Gotama.
Dhamman, tenet, doctrine, custom, law, religion, virtue, thing.
Gahattha, Gihin, a householder.
Gotama, a name of the last Buddha.
Jatila, an ascetic weari8ng clotted hair.
Jina, a conqueror, a name of a Buddha.
Isi, a sage.
Kshatriya Kattiya, rishi a warrior, a prince.
Mara, a name of the king of death, the devil.
Muni, sage.
Naga, an eminent man.
Namuch = Mara.
Nibbana, extinction, the state of bliss of the Buddhist.
Nigantha, a naked ascetic.
Pabbajja, leaving the world, embracing ascetic life, taking the robe.
Pabbajita, an ascetic, having taken the robe.
Paribbaja, Paribbajaka, a wandering mendicant.
Sakka=Sakya, belonging to the Sakya race, a name of Buddha.
Samana, an ascetic.
Samkhara, all compound things, the material world, the elements of existence.
Samsara, revolution, transmigratioin.
Savaka, a hearer, a follower, a disciple of Buddha, including both laity and clergy.
Sekha, a novice, student.
Suddha, Shudra, a man of the servile caste.
Sugata, happy, a name of Buddha.
Thera, an elder, a senior priest.
Titthiya, an ascetic adhering to a certain system of philosophy.
Upadhi, the elements of the world.
Upasaka, a follower, a lay devotee.
Upasampada, priest's orders.
Vessa, Vessika, a man of the third caste, Vaishya.
Yakkha, a giant, a malignant spirit.

Contents

The Snake Section (Uragavagga)

The Small Section (Chulavagga)

The Large Section (Mahavagga)

Dhamekha Stupa at Sarnath, where Lord Buddha gave his first sermon.

First Sermon at Sarnath, Cave 4

1

The Snake Section

(Uragavagga)

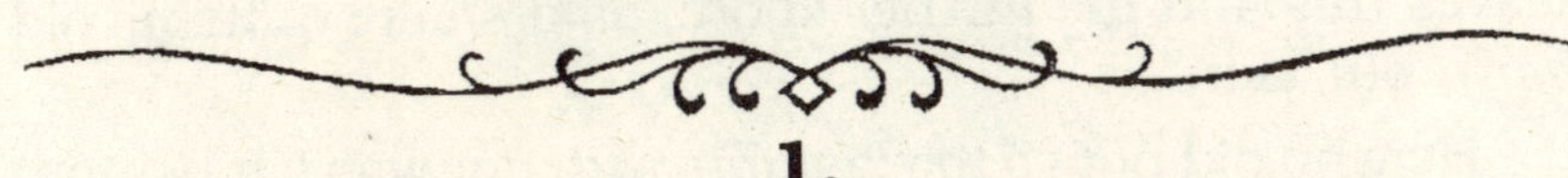

1.

Quit as a Snake Your Worn Out Skin

The Bhikkhu who discards all human passions is compared to a snake that casts his skin.

He who restrains his anger when it has arisen, as they by medicines restrain the poison of the snake spreading in the body, that Bhikkhu leaves this and the further shore, as a snake quits its old worn out skin.

He who has cut off passion entirely, as they cut off the lotus-flower growing in a lake, after diving into the water, that Bhikkhu leaves this and the further shore, as a snake quits its old worn out skin.

He who has cut off craving entirely, the flowing, the quickly running, after drying it up, that Bhikkhu leaves this and the further shore, as a snake quits its old worn out skin.

He who has destroyed arrogance entirely, as the flood destroys a very frail bridge of reeds, that Bhikkhu leaves this and the further shore, as a snake quits its old worn out skin.

He who has not found any essence in the existences, like one that looks for flowers on fig-trees, that Bhikkhu leaves this and the further shore, as a snake quits its old worn out skin.

He in whose breast there are no feelings of anger, who has thus overcome reiterated existence, that Bhikkhu leaves this and the further shore, as a snake quits its old worn out skin.

He whose doubts are scattered, cut off entirely inwardly, that Bhikkhu leaves this and the further shore, as a snake quits its old worn out skin.

He who did not go too fast forward, nor was left behind, who overcame all this world of delusion, that Bhikkhu leaves this and the further shore, as a snake quits its old worn out skin.

He who did not go too fast forward, nor was left behind, having seen that all this in the world is false, that Bhikkhu leaves this and the further shore, as a snake quits its old worn out skin.

He who did not go too fast forward, nor was left behind, being free from covetousness, seeing that all this is false, that Bhikkhu leaves this and the further shore, as a snake quits its old worn out skin.

He who did not go too fast forward, nor was left behind, being free from passion, seeing that all this is false, that Bhikkhu leaves this and the further shore, as a snake quits its old worn out skin.

He who did not go too fast forward, nor was left behind, being free from hatred, seeing that all this is false, that Bhikkhu leaves this and the further shore, as a snake quits its old worn out skin.

He who did not go too fast forward, nor was left behind, being free from folly, seeing that all this is false, that Bhikkhu leaves this and the further shore, as a snake quits its old worn out skin.

He to whom there are no affections whatsoever, whose sins are extirpated from the root, that Bhikkhu leaves this and the further shore, as a snake quits its old worn out skin.

He to whom there are no sins whatsoever, originating in fear, which are the causes of coming back to this shore, that Bhikkhu leaves this and the further shore, as a snake quits its old worn out skin.

He to whom there are no sins whatsoever originating in desire, which are the causes of binding men to existence, that Bhikkhu leaves this and the further shore, as a snake quits its old worn out skin.

He who, having left the five obstacles, is free from suffering, has overcome doubt, and is without pain, that Bhikkhu leaves this and the further shore, as a snake quits its old worn out skin.

2.

If thou like, rain, O Sky!

(Dhaniya Sutta)

A dialogue between the rich herdsman Dhaniya and Buddha, the one rejoicing in his worldly security and the other in his religious belief.

'I have boiled my rice, I have milked my cows '— so said the herdsman Dhaniya,—'I am living together with my fellows near the banks of the Mahi river, my house is covered, the fire is kindled: therefore, if thou like, rain, O sky!'

'I am free from anger, free from stubbornness,'—so said Bhagavat,—' I am abiding for one night near the banks of the Mahi river, my house is uncovered, the fire of passions is extinguished: therefore, if thou like, rain, O sky!'

'Gadflies are not to be found with me,'—so said the herdsman Dhaniya,— 'in meadows abounding with grass the cows are roaming, and they can endure rain when it comes: therefore, if thou like, rain, O sky!'

'By me is made a well-constructed raft,'—so said Bhagavat,— 'I have passed over to Nibbana, I have reached the further bank, having overcome the torrent of passions; there is no further use for a raft: therefore, if thou like, rain, O sky!'

'My wife is obedient, not wanton,'—so said the herdsman Dhaniya,—' for a long time she has been living together, with me she is winning, and I hear nothing wicked of her: therefore, if thou like, rain, O sky!'

'My mind is obedient, delivered from all worldliness,'—so said Bhagavat,—'it has for a long time been highly cultivated and well-subdued, there is no longer anything wicked in me: therefore, if thou like, rain, O sky!'

'I support myself by my own earnings,'—so said the herdsman Dhaniya.—'and my children are all about me, healthy; I hear nothing wicked of them: therefore, if thou like, rain, O sky!'

'I am no one's servant,'—so said Bhagavat,—'with what I have gained I wander about in all the world, there is no need for me to serve: therefore, if thou like, rain, O sky!'

'I have cows, I have calves,'—so said the herdsman Dhaniya,—'I have cows in calf and heifers, and I have also a bull as lord over the cows: therefore, if thou like, rain, O sky!'

'I have no cows, I have no calves,'—so said Bhagavat, — 'I have no cows in calf and heifers, and I have no bull as a lord over the cows: therefore, if thou like, rain, O sky!'

'The stakes are driven in, and cannot be shaken,'—so said the herdsman Dhaniya,—'the ropes are made of *munja* grass, new and well-made, the cows will not be of able to break them: therefore, if thou like, rain, O sky!'

'Having, like a bull, rent the bonds; having, like an elephant, broken through the *galuchchi* creeper, I shall not again enter into a womb: therefore, if thou like, rain, O sky!'

Then at once a shower poured down, filling both sea and land. Hearing the sky raining, Dhaniya spoke thus:

'No small gain indeed has accrued to us since we have seen Bhagavat; we take refuge in thee, O thou who art

Celestial Musicians, Cave 17

endowed with the eye of wisdom; be thou our master, O great Muni!

'Both my wife and myself are obedient; if we lead a holy life before Sugata, we shall conquer birth and death, and put an end to pain.'

'He who has sons has delight in sons,'—so said the wicked Mara,— 'he who has cows has delight likewise in cows; for Upadhi (substance) is the delight of man, but he who has no Upadhi has no delight.'

'He who has sons has care with his sons,'—so said Bhagavat,—'he who has cows has likewise care with his cows; for Upadhi is the cause of people's cares, but he who has no Upadhi has no care.'

3.

Wander Alone Like a Rhinoceros

(Khaggavisana Sutta)

Family life and relations with others should be avoided, for society has all vices in its train; therefore one should leave the corrupted state of society and lead a solitary life.

Having laid aside the rod against all beings, and not hurting any of them, let no one wish for a son, much less for a companion, let him wander alone like a rhinoceros.

In him who has relations with others affections arise, and then the pain which follows affection; considering the misery that originates in affection, let one wander alone like a rhinoceros.

He who has compassion on his friends and confidential companions loses his own advantage, having a fettered mind; seeing this danger in friendship, let one wander alone like a rhinoceros.

Just as a large bamboo tree with its branches entangled in each other, such is the care one has with children and wife; but like the shoot of a bamboo not clinging to anything, let one wander alone like a rhinoceros.

As a beast unbound in the forest goes feeding at pleasure, so let the wise man, considering only his own will, wander alone like a rhinoceros.

There is a constant calling in the midst of company, both when sitting, standing, walking, and going away; but let one, looking only for freedom from desire and for following his own will, wander alone like a rhinoceros.

There is sport and amusement in the midst of company, and for children there is great affection; although disliking separation from his dear friends, let one wander alone like a rhinoceros.

He who is at home in all the four regions and is not hostile to any one, being content with this or that, overcoming all dangers fearlessly, let him wander alone like a rhinoceros.

Discontented are some ascetics, also some householders dwelling in houses; let one, caring little about other people's children, wander alone like a rhinoceros.

Removing the marks of a householder like a Kovilara tree whose leaves are fallen, let one, after cutting off heroically the ties of a time, wander alone like a rhinoceros.

If one acquires a clever companion, an associate righteous and wise, let him, overcoming all dangers, wander about with him glad and thoughtful.

If one does not acquire a clever companion, an associate righteous and wise, then as a king abandoning his conquered kingdom, let him wander alone like a rhinoceros.

Surely we ought to praise the good luck of having companions, the best and such as are our equals ought to be sought for; not having acquired such friends, let one, enjoying only allowable things, wander alone like a rhinoceros.

Seeing bright golden bracelets, well-wrought by the goldsmith, striking against each other when there are two on one arm, let one wander alone like a rhinoceros.

Thus if I join myself with another I shall swear or scold; considering this danger in future, let one wander alone like a rhinoceros.

The sensual pleasures indeed, which are various, sweet, and charming, under their different shapes agitate the mind; seeing the misery originating in sensual pleasures, let one wander alone like a rhinoceros.

These pleasures are to me calamities, boils, misfortunes, diseases, sharp pains, and dangers; seeing this danger originating in sensual pleasures, let one wander alone like a rhinoceros.

Both cold and heat, hunger and thirst, wind and a burning sun, and gadflies and snakes—having overcome all these things, let one wander alone like a rhinoceros.

As the elephant, the strong, the spotted, the large, after leaving the herd walks at pleasure in the forest, even so, let one wander alone like a rhinoceros.

For him who delights in intercourse with others, even that is inconvenient which tends to temporary deliverance; reflecting on the words of Buddha the kinsman of the Adichcha family, let one wander alone like a rhinoceros.

The harshness of the philosophical views I have overcome, I have acquired self-command, I have attained to the way leading to perfection, I am in possession of knowledge, and not to be led by others; so speaking, let one wander alone like a rhinoceros.

Without covetousness, without deceit, without craving, without detraction, having got rid of passions and folly, being free from desire in all the world, let one wander alone like a rhinoceros.

Let one avoid a wicked companion who teaches what is useless and has gone into what is wrong, let him not cultivate the society of one who is devoted to and lost in sensual pleasures, let one wander alone like a rhinoceros.

Let one cultivate the society of a friend who is learned and keeps the Dhamma, who is magnanimous and wise; knowing the meaning of things and subduing his doubts, let one wander alone like a rhinoceros.

Not adorning himself, not looking out for sport, amusement, and the delight of pleasure in the world, on the contrary, being loath of a life of dressing, speaking the truth, let one wander alone like a rhinoceros.

Having left son and wife, father and mother, wealth and corn, and relatives, the different objects of desire, let one wander alone like a rhinoceros.

'This is a tie, in this there is little happiness, little enjoyment, but more of pain, this is a fish-hook,' so having understood, let a thoughtful man wander alone like a rhinoceros.

Having torn the ties, having broken the net as a fish in the water, being like a fire not returning to the burnt place, let one wander alone like a rhinoceros.

With downcast eyes, and not prying, with his senses guarded, with his mind protected free from passion, not burning with lust, let one wander alone like a rhinoceros.

Removing the characteristics of a householder, like a Parichhatta tree whose leaves are cut off, clothed in a yellow robe after wandering away from his house, let one wander alone like a rhinoceros.

Not being greedy of sweet things, not being unsteady, not supporting others, going begging from house to house, having a mind which is not fettered to any household, let one wander alone like a rhinoceros.

Having left the five obstacles of the mind having dispelled all sin, being independent, having cut off the sin of desire, let one wander alone like a rhinoceros.

Having thrown behind himself bodily pleasure and pain, and previously mental joy and distress, having acquired equanimity, tranquillity, purity, let one wander alone like a rhinoceros.

Strenuous for obtaining the supreme good Nibbana, with a mind free from attachment, not living in idleness, being firm, endowed with bodily and mental strength, let one wander alone like a rhinoceros.

Not abandoning seclusion and meditation, always wandering in accordance with the Dhammas, seeing misery in the existences, let one wander alone like a rhinoceros.

Wishing for the destruction of desire, Nibbana, being careful, no fool, learned, strenuous, considerate, restrained, energetic, let one wander alone like a rhinoceros.

Like a lion not trembling at noises, like the wind not caught in a net, like a lotus not stained by water, let one wander alone like a rhinoceros.

As a lion strong by his teeth, after overcoming all animals, wanders victorious as the king of the animals, and haunts distant dwelling-places, even so let one wander alone like a rhinoceros.

Cultivating in due time kindness, equanimity, compassion, deliverance, and rejoicing with others, unobstructed by the whole world, let one wander alone like a rhinoceros.

Having abandoned both passion and hatred and folly, having rent the ties, not trembling in the loss of life, let one wander alone like a rhinoceros.

They cultivate the society of others and serve them for the sake of advantage; friends without a motive are now difficult to get, men know their own profit and are impure; therefore, let one wander alone like a rhinoceros.

4.

'Plough and Sow, Gotama, to Eat'

(Kasibharadvaja Sutta)

The Brahmin Kasibharadvaja reproaches Gotama with idleness, but the latter convinces him that he (Buddha) also works, and so the Brahmin is converted, and finally becomes a saint.

So it was heard by me:

At one time Bhagavat dwelt in Magadha at Dakkhinagiri in the Brahmin village Ekanala. And at that time the

Brahmin Kasibharadvaja's five hundred ploughs were tied to the yokes in the sowing season. Then Bhagavat, in the morning, having put on his raiment and taken his bowl and robes, went to the place where the Brahmin Kasibharadvaja's work was going on. At that time the Brahmin Kasibharadvaja's distribution of food took place. Then Bhagavat went to the place where the distribution of food took place, and having gone there, he stood apart. The Brahmin Kasibharadvaja saw Bhagavat standing there to get alms, and having seen him, he said this to Bhagavat:

'I, O Samana, both plough and sow, and having ploughed and sown, I eat; thou also, O Samana, shouldst plough and sow, and having ploughed and sown, thou shouldst eat.'

'I also, O Brahmin, both plough and sow, and having ploughed and sown, I eat,' so said Bhagavat.

'Yet we do not see the yoke, or the plough, or the ploughshare, or the goad, or the oxen of the venerable Gotama.'

And then the venerable Gotama spoke in this way:

'I also, O Brahmin, both plough and sow, and having ploughed and sown, I eat,' so said Bhagavat.

Then the Brahmin Kasibharadvaja addressed Bhagavat in a stanza:

'Thou prcfessest to be a ploughman, and yet we do not see thy ploughing; asked about thy ploughing, tell us of it, that we may know thy ploughing.'

Bhagavat answered: 'Faith is the seed, penance the rain, understanding my yoke and plough, modesty the pole plough, mind the tie, thoughtfulness my plouhghshare and goad.

'I am guarded in respect of the body, I am guarded in respect of speech, temperate in food; I make truth to cut away weeds, tenderness is my deliverance.

'Exertion is my beast of burden; carrying me to Nibbana he goes without turning back to the place where having gone one does not grieve.

'So this ploughing is ploughed, it bears the fruit of immortality; having ploughed this ploughing one is freed from all pain.'

Then the Brahmin Kasibharadvaja, having poured rice-milk into a golden bowl, offered it to Bhagavat, saying, 'Let the venerable Bhagavat eat of the rice-milk; the venerable is a ploughman, for the venerable Gotama ploughs a ploughing that bears the fruit of immortality.'

Bhagavat said: 'What is acquired by reciting stanzas is not to be eaten by me; this is, O Brahmin, not the Dhamma of those that see rightly; Buddha rejects what is acquired by reciting stanzas, this is the conduct of Buddhas as long as the Dhamma exists.

'One who is an accomplished great Isi (Rishi), whose passions are destroyed and whose misbehaviour has ceased, thou shouldst serve with other food and drink, for this is the field for one who looks for good works.'

'To whom then, O Gotama, shall I give this rice-milk?' so said Kasibharadvaja.

'I do not see, O Brahmin, in the world of men and gods and Maras and Brahmins, amongst beings comprising gods and men, and Samanas and Brahmins, any by whom this rice-milk when eaten can be properly digested with the exception of Tathagata, or a disciple of Tathagata. Therefore, O Brahmin, thou shalt throw this rice-milk in a place where there is little grass, or cast it into water with no worms,' so said Bhagavat.

Then the Brahmin Kasibharadvaja threw the rice-milk into some water with no worms. Then the rice-milk thrown into the water splashed, hissed, smoked in volumes; for as a ploughshare that has got hot during the day when thrown into the water splashes, hisses, and smokes in volumes, even so the rice-milk when thrown into the water splashed, hissed, and smoked in volumes.

Then the Brahmin Kasibharadvaja alarmed and terrified went up to Bhagavat, and after having approached and fallen with his head at Bhagavat's feet, he said this to Bhagavat:

'It is excellent, O venerable Gotama! It is excellent, O venerable Gotama! As one raises what has been overthrown, or reveals what has been hidden, or tells the way to him who has gone astray, or holds out an oil lamp in the dark that those who have eyes may see the objects, even so by the venerable Gotama in manifold ways the Dhamma has been illustrated. I take refuge in the venerable Gotama and in the Dhamma and in the Sangh of Bhikkhus; I wish to receive the Pabbajja, I wish to receive the Upasampada (the robe and the orders) from the venerable Gotama,' so said Kasibharadvaja.

Then the Brahmin Kasibharadvaja received the Pabbajja from Bhagavat, and he received also the Upasampada; and the venerable Bharadvaja having lately received the Upasampada, leading a solitary, retired, strenuous, ardent, energetic life, lived after having in a short time in this existence by his own understanding ascertained and possessed himself of that highest perfection of a religious life for the sake of which men of good family rightly wander away from their houses to a houseless state. 'Birth had been destroyed, a religious life had been led, what was to be done had been done, there was nothing else to be done for this existence,' so he perceived, and the venerable Bharadvaja became one of the arahats.

5.
Samanas Are of Four Kinds
(Chunda Sutta)

Buddha describes the four different kinds of Samanas to Chunda, the smith.

'I ask the Muni of great understanding,' —so said Chunda, the smith,—'Buddha, the lord of the Dhamma, who is free from craving, the best of bipeds, the most excellent of charioteers, how many kinds of Samanas are there in the world; pray tell me that?'

'There are four kinds of Samanas, there is not a fifth, O Chunda,' —so said Bhagavat,—'these I will reveal to thee, being asked in person; they are Maggjinas and Maggadesakas, Maggajivins and Maggadusins.'

'Whom do the Buddhas call a Maggjina?' — so said Chunda, the smith,—'How is a Maggajjhayin unequalled? Being asked, describe to me a Maggajivin, and reveal to me a Maggadusin.'

Bhagavat said: 'He who has overcome doubt, is without pain, delights in Nibbana, is free from greed, a leader of the world of men and gods, such a one the Buddhas call a Maggajina, that is, victorious by the way.

'He who in this world having known the best, Nibbana as the best, expounds and explains here the Dhamma, him, the doubt-cutting Muni, without desire, the second Bhikkhu they call a Maggadesin, that is, teaching the way.

'He who lives in the way that has so well been taught in the Dhammapada, and is restrained, attentive, cultivating blameless words, him the third Bhikkhu they call a Maggajivin, that is, living in the way.

'He who although counterfeiting the virtuous is forward, disgraces families, is impudent, deceitful, unrestrained, a babbler, walking in disguise, such a one is a Maggadusin, that is, defiling the way.

'He who has penetrated these four Samanas, who is a householder, possessed of knowledge, a pupil of the venerable ones, wise, having known that they all are such, —having seen so, his faith is not lost; for how could he make the undepraved equal to the depraved and the pure equal to the impure?'

Tallest Buddha Statwe in the World. 71m.
At the confluence of rivers Min and Dada,
in Sechuan Province, China.

6.

Why Does a Man Lose, or Gain?

(Parabhava Sutta)

A dialogue between a deity and Buddha on the things by which a man loses and those by which he gains in this world.

So it was heard by me:

At one time Bhagavat dwelt at Savatthi, in Jetavana, in the park of Anathapindika. Then when the night had come, a certain deity of a beautiful appearance, having illuminated the whole Jetavana, went up to Bhagavat, and having approached and saluted him, he stood apart, and standing apart that deity addressed Bhagavat in stanzas:

'We ask thee, Gotama, about a man that suffers loss; having come to ask, Bhagavat, tell us what is the cause of loss to the losing man.'

Bhagavat: 'The winner is easily known, easily known is also the loser: he who loves Dhamma is the winner, he who hates Dhamma is the loser.'

Deity: 'We know this to be so, this is the first loser; tell us the second, O Bhagavat, what is the cause of loss to the losing man.'

Bhagavat: 'Wicked men are dear to him, he does not do anything that is dear to the good, he approves of the Dhamma of the wicked, —that is the cause of loss to the losing man.'

Deity: 'We know this to be so, this is the second loser; tell us the third, O Bhagavat, what is the cause of loss to the losing man.'

Bhagavat: 'The man who is drowsy, fond of society and without energy, lazy, given to anger, —that is the cause of loss to the losing man.'

Deity: 'We know this to be so, this is the third loser; tell us the fourth, O Bhagavat, what is the cause of loss to the losing man?

Bhagavat: 'He who, being rich does not support mother or father who are old or past their youth,—that is the cause of loss to the losing man.'

Deity: 'We know this to be so, this is the fourth loser; tell us the fifth, O Bhagavat, what is the cause of loss to the losing man.'

Bhagavat: 'He who by falsehood deceives either a Brahmin or a Samana or any other mendicant,—that is the cause of loss to the losing man.'

Deity: 'We know this to be so, this is the fifth loser; tell us the sixth, O Bhagavat, what is the cause of loss to the losing man?'

Bhagavat: 'The man who is possessed of much property, who has gold and food, and still enjoys alone his sweet things,—that is the cause of loss to the losing man.'

Deity: 'We know this to be so, this is the sixth loser; tell us the seventh, O Bhagavat, what is the cause of loss to the losing man?'

Bhagavat: 'The man who, proud of his birth, of his wealth, and of his family, despises his relatives,—that is the cause of loss to the losing man.'

Deity: 'We know this to be so, this is the seventh loser; tell us the eighth, O Bhagavat, what is the cause of loss to the losing man.'

Bhagavat: 'The man who, given to women, to strong drink, and to dice, wastes whatever he has gained—that is the cause of loss to the losing man.'

Deity: 'We know this to be so, this is the eighth loser; tell us the ninth, O Bhagavat, what is the cause of loss to the losing man.'

Bhagavat: 'He who, not satisfied with his own wife, is seen with harlots and the wives of others,—that is the cause of loss to the losing man.'

Deity: 'We know this to be so, this is the ninth loser; tell us the tenth, O Bhagavat, what is the cause of loss to the losing man.'

Bhagavat: The man who, past his youth, brings home a woman with breasts like the *tumbaru* fruit, and for jealousy of her cannot sleep,—that is the cause of loss to the losing man.'

Deity: 'We know this to be so, this is the tenth loser; tell us the eleventh, O Bhagavat, what is the cause of loss to the losing man.'

Bhagavat: 'He who places in supremacy a woman given to drink and squandering, or a man of the same kind,—that is the cause of loss to the losing man.'

Deity: 'We know this to be so, this is the eleventh loser; tell us the twelfth, O Bhagavat, what is the cause of loss to the losing man.'

Bhagavat: 'He who has little property, but great craving, is born in a Khattiya family and wishes for the kingdom in this world,—that is the cause of loss to the losing man.

Having taken into consideration these losses in the world, the wise, venerable man, who is endowed with insight, cultivates the happy world of the gods.

7.

What Makes One an Outcast?

(Vasala Sutta)

The Brahmin Aggikabharadvaja is converted by Buddha, after hearing his definition of an outcast, illustrated by the story of Matanga, told in the Matangajataka.

So it was heard by me:

At one time Bhagavat dwelt at Savatthi, in Jetavana, in the park of Anathapindika. Then Bhagavat having put on his raiment in the morning, and having taken his bowl and his robes, entered Savatthi for alms.

Now at that time in the house of the Brahmin Aggikabharadavja the fire was blazing, the offering brought forth. Then Bhagavat going for alms from house to house in Savatthi went to the house of the Brahmin

Aggikabharadvaja. The Brahmin Aggikabharadvaja saw Bhagavat coming at a distance, and seeing him he said this: 'Stay there, O Shaveling; stay there, O Samanaka (wretched Samana); stay there, O Vasalaka (outcast)!'

This having been said, Bhagavat replied to the Brahmin Aggikabharadvaja: 'Dost thou know, O Brahmin, an outcast, or the things that make an outcast?'

'No, O venerable Gotama, I do not know an outcast, or the things that make an outcast; let the venerable Gotama teach me this so well that I may know an outcast, or the things that make an outcast.'

'Listen then, O Brahmin, attend carefully, I will tell thee.'

'Even so, O venerable one,' so the Brahmin Aggikabharadvaja replied to Bhagvat.

Then Bhagavat said this:

'The man who is angry and bears hatred, who is wicked and hypocritical, who has embraced wrong views, who is deceitful, let one know him as an outcast.

'Whosoever in this world harms living beings, whether once or twice born, and in whom there is no compassion for living beings, let one know him as an outcast.

'Whosoever destroys or lays siege to villages and towns, and is known as an enemy, let one know him as an outcast.

'Be it in the village or in the wood, whosoever appropriates by theft what is the property of others and what has not been given, let one know him as an outcast.

'Whosoever, having really contracted a debt, runs away when caned upon to pay, saying, "There is no debt that I owe thee," let one know him as an outcast.

'Whosoever for love of a trifle having killed a man going along the road, takes the trifle, let one know him as an outcast.

'The man who for his own sake or for that of others or for the sake of wealth speaks falsely when asked as a witness, let one know him as an outcast.

'Whosoever is seen with the wives of relatives or of friends either by force or with their consent, let one know him as an outcast.

'Whosoever being rich does not support mother or father when old and past their youth, let one know him as an outcast.

'Whosoever strikes or by words annoys mother or father, brother, sister, or mother-in-law, let one know him as an outcast.

'Whosoever, being asked about what is good, teaches what is bad and advises another, while concealing something from him, let one know him as an outcast.

'Whosoever, having committed a bad deed, hopes saying, "Let no one know me" as having done it, who is a dissembler, let one know him as an outcast.

'Whosoever, having gone to another's house and partaken of his good food, does not in return honour him when he comes, let one know him as an outcast.

'Whosoever by falsehood deceives either a Brahmin or a Samana or any other mendicant, let one know him as an outcast.

'Whosoever by words annoys either a Brahmin or a Samana when meal-time has come and does not give him anything, let one know him as an outcast.

'Whosoever enveloped in ignorance in this world predicts what is not to take place, coveting a trifle, let one know him as an outcast.

'Whosoever exalts himself and despises others, being mean by his pride, let one know him as an outcast.

'Whosoever is a provoker and is avaricious, has sinful desires, is envious, wicked, shameless, and fearless of sinning, let one know him as an outcast.

'Whosoever reviles Buddha or his disciples, be he a wandering mendicant or a householder, let one know him as an outcast.

'Whosoever without being a saint (arahat) pretends to be a saint, and is a thief in all the worlds including that of Brahman, he is indeed the lowest outcast; all these who have been described by me to you are indeed called outcasts.

'Not by birth does one become an outcast, not by birth does one become a Brahmin; by deeds one becomes an outcast, by deeds one becomes a Brahmin.

'Know ye this in the way that this example of mine shows: There was a Chandala of the Sopaka caste, well known as Matanga.

'This Matanga reached the highest fame, such as was very difficult to obtain, and many Khattiyas and Brahmins went to serve him.

'He having mounted the vehicle of the gods, and entered the high road that is free from dust, having abandoned sensual desires, went to the Brahma world.

'His birth did not prevent him from being reborn in the Brahma world; on the other hand, there are Brahmins, born in the family of preceptors, friends of the hymns of the Vedas.

'But they are continually caught in sinful deeds, and are to be blamed in this world, while in the coming world hell awaits them; birth does not save them from hell nor from blame.

'Therefore, not by birth does one become an outcast not by birth does one become a Brahmin, by deeds one becomes an outcast, by deeds one becomes a Brahmin.'

This having been said, the Brahmin Aggikabharadvaja answered Bhagavat as follows:

'Excellent, O venerable Gotama! Excellent, O venerable Gotama! As one, O venerable Gotama, raises what has been overthrown, or reveals what has been hidden, or tells the way to him who has gone astray, or holds out an oil lamp in the dark that those who have eyes may see the objects, even so by the venerable Gotama in manifold ways the Ðhamma has been illustrated; I take refuge in the venerable Gotama and in the Dhamma and in the Sangh of Bhikkhus. Let the venerable Gotama accept me as a follower, me who henceforth for all my life have taken refuge in him.'

8.

The Best Way of Living in the World

(Metta Sutta)

A peaceful mind and goodwill towards all beings are praised.

Whatever is to be done by one who is skilful in seeking what is good, having attained that tranquil state of Nibbana— Let him be able and upright and conscientious and of soft speech, gentle, not proud,

And contented and easily supported and having few cares, unburdened and with his senses calmed and wise, not arrogant, without showing greediness when going his round in families.

And let him not do anything mean for which others who are wise might reprove him; may all beings be happy and secure, may they be happy-minded.

Whatever living beings there are, either feeble or strong, either long or great, middle-sized, short, small or large,

Either seen or which are not seen, and which live far or near, either born or seeking birth, may all creatures be happy-minded.

Let no one deceive another, let him not despise another in any place, let him not out of anger or resentment wish harm to another.

As a mother at the risk of her life watches over her own child, her only child, so also let every one cultivate a boundless friendly mind towards all beings.

And let him cultivate goodwill towards all the world, a boundless friend by mind, above and below and across, unobstructed, without hatred, without enmity.

Bodhistattva Padmapani, Cave 1

Standing, walking or sitting or lying, as long as he be awake, let him devote himself to this mind; this way of living they say is the best in this world.

He who, not having embraced philosophical views, is virtuous, endowed with perfect vision, after subduing greediness for sensual pleasures, will never again go to a mother's womb.

9.
By What Is the World Afflicted
(Hemavata Sutta)

A dialogue between two Yakkhas on the qualities of Buddha. They go to Buddha, and after having their questions answered they, together with ten hundred Yakkhas, become the followers of Buddha.

'Today is the fifteenth, a fast day; a lovely night has come,' —so said the Yakkha Satagira,—'let us go and see the renowned Master Gotama.'

'Is the mind of such a one well disposed towards all beings?' —so said the Yakkha Hemavata,—'are his thoughts restrained as to things wished for or not wished for?'

'His mind is well disposed towards all beings, the mind of such a one,' —so said the Yakkha Satagira,—'and his thoughts are restrained as to things wished for or not wished for.'

'Does he not take what has not been given to him?' —so said the Yakkha Hemavata,—'is he self-controlled in his behaviour to living beings? is he far from a state of carelessness? does he not abandon meditation?'

'He does not take what has not been given to him,' —so said the Yakkha Satagira,—'and he is self-controlled in his behaviour to living beings, and he is far from a state of carelessness; Buddha does not abandon meditation.'

'Does he not speak falsely?'—so said the Yakkha Hemavata,—'is he not harsh-spoken? does he not utter slander? does he not talk nonsense?'

'He does not speak falsely,'—so said the Yakkha Satagira,—'he is not harsh-spoken, he does not utter slander, with judgment he utters what is good sense.'

'Is he not given to sensual pleasures?'—so said the Yakkha Hemavata,—'is his mind undisturbed? has he overcome folly? does he see clearly in all things?'

'He is not given to sensual pleasures,'—so said the Yakkha Satagira,—'and his mind is undisturbed; he has overcome all folly; Buddha sees clearly in all things.'

'Is he endowed with knowledge?'—so said the Yakkha Hemavata,—'is his conduct pure? have his passions been destroyed? is there no new birth for him?'

'He is endowed with knowledge,'—so said the Yakkha Satagira,'—and his conduct is pure; all his passions have been destroyed; there is no new birth for him.

'The mind of the Muni is accomplished in deed and word; Gotama, who is accomplished by his knowledge and conduct, let us go and see.

'Come, let us go and see Gotama, who has legs like an antelope, who is thin, who is wise, living on little food, not covetous, the Muni who is meditating in the forest.

'Having gone to him who is like a lion, a lonely wandering elephant, and who does not look for sensual pleasures, let us ask about the means of deliverance from the snares of death.

'Let us ask Gotama, the preacher, the expounder, who has penetrated all things, Buddha, who has overcome hatred and fear.'

'In what has the world originated?'—so said the Yakkha Hemavata—'with what is the world intimate? by what is the world afflicted, after having grasped at what?'

'In six sins the world has originated, O Hemavata,'—so said Bhagavat,—'with six it is intimate, by six the world is afflicted, after having grasped at six.'

Hemavata said: 'What is the grasping by which the world is afflicted? Asked about salvation, tell me how one is released from pain?'

Bhagavat said: 'Five pleasures of sense are said to be in the world, with the pleasure of the mind as the sixth; having divested oneself of desire for these, one is thus released from pain.

'This salvation of the world has been told to you truly, this I tell you: thus one is released from pain.'

Hemavata said: 'Who in this world crosses the stream of existence? who in this world crosses the sea? who does not sink into the deep, where there is no footing and no support?'

Bhagavat said: 'He who is always endowed with virtue, possessed of understanding, well composed, reflecting within himself, and thoughtful, crosses the stream that is difficult to cross.

'He who is disgusted with sensual pleasures, who has overcome all bonds and destroyed joy, such a one does not sink into the deep.'

Hemavata said: 'He who is endowed with a profound understanding, seeing what is subtle, possessing nothing, not clinging to sensual pleasures, behold him who is in every respect liberated, the great Isi, walking in the divine path.

'He who has got a great name, sees what is subtle, imparts understanding, and does not cling to the abode of sensual pleasures, behold him, the all-knowing, the wise, the great Isi, walking in the noble path.

'A good sight indeed has met us today, a good daybreak, a beautiful rising, for we have seen the perfectly enlightened (sambaddham), who has crossed the stream, and is free from passion.

'These ten hundred Yakkhas, possessed of supernatural power and of fame, they all take refuge in thee, thou art our incomparable Master.

'We will wander about from village to village, from mountain to mountain, worshipping the perfectly enlightened and the perfection of the Dhamma they call.'

10

How Lived Is Life the Best?

(Alavaka Sutta)

The Yakkha Alavaka first threatens Buddha, then puts some questions to him which Buddha answers, whereupon Alavaka is converted.

So it was heard by me:

At one time Bhagavat dwelt at Alavi, in the realm of the Yakkha Alavaka. Then the Yakkha Alavaka went to the place where Bhagavat dwelt, and having gone there he said this to Bhagavat:

'Come out, O Samana!'

'Yes, O friend! so saying Bhagavat came out.

'Enter, O Samana!'

'Yes, O friend!' so saying Bhagavat entered.

A second time the Yakkha Alavaka said this to Bhagavat: 'Come out, O Samana!'

'Yes, O friend!' so saying Bhagavat came out.

'Enter, O Samana!'

'Yes, O friend!' so saying Bhagavat entered.

A third time the Yakkha Alavaka said this to Bhagavat: 'Come out, O Samana !'

'Yes, O friend!' so saying Bhagavat came out.

'Enter, O Samana!'

'Yes, O friend!' so saying Bhagavat entered.

A fourth time the Yakkha Alavaka said this to Bhagavat: 'Come out, O Samana!'

'I shall not come out to thee, O friend, do what thou pleasest.'

'I shall ask thee a question, O Samana, if thou canst answer it, I will either scatter thy thoughts or cleave thy heart, or take thee by thy feet and throw thee over *to* the other shore of the Ganga.'

'I do not see, O friend, anyone in this world nor in the world of gods, Maras, Brahmins, amongst the beings comprising gods, men, Samanas, and Brahmins, who can either scatter my thoughts or cleave my heart, or take me by the feet and throw me over to the other shore of the Ganga; however, O friend, ask what thou pleasest.'

Then the Yakkha Alavaka addressed Bhagavat in stanzas:

'What in this world is the best property for a man? what, being well done, conveys happiness? what is indeed the sweetest of sweet things? how lived do they call life the best?'

Bhagavat said: 'Faith is in this world the best property for a man; Dhamma, well observed, conveys happiness; truth indeed is the sweetest of things; and that life they call the best which is lived with understanding.'

Alavaka said: 'How does one cross the stream of existence? how does one cross the sea? how does one conquer pain? how is one purified?'

Bhagavat said: 'By faith one crosses the stream, by zeal the sea, by exertion one conquers pain, by understanding one is purified.'

Alavaka said: 'How does one obtain understanding? how does one acquire wealth? how does one obtain fame? how does one bind friends to himself? how does one not grieve passing away from this world to the other?'

Bhagavat said: 'He who believes in the Dhamma of the venerable ones as to the acquisition of Nibbana, will obtain understanding from his desire to hear, being zealous and discerning.

'He who does what is proper, who takes the yoke upon him and exerts himself, will acquire wealth: by truth he will obtain fame, and being charitable he will bind friends to himself.

'He who is faithful and leads the life of a householder, and possesses the following four Dhammas; truth, justice firmness, and liberality,—such a one indeed does not grieve when passing away.

'Pray, ask also other Samanas and Brahmins far and wide, whether there is found in this world anything greater than truth, self-restraint, liberality, and forbearance.'

Alavaka said:, Why should I now ask Samanas and Brahmins far and wide? I now know what is my future good.

'For my good Buddha came to live at Alavi; now I know on whom bestowed a gift will bear great fruit.

'I will wander about from village to village, from town to town, worshipping the perfectly enlightened and the perfection of the Dhamma.'

11.

The Body—Impure, Filled with Stench

(Vijaya Sutta)

A reflection on the worthlessness of the human body; a follower of Buddha only sees the body as it really is, and consequently goes to Nibbana.

If either walking or standing, sitting or lying, anyone contracts or stretches his body, then this is the motion of the body.

The body which is put together with bones and sinews, plastered with membrane and flesh, and covered with skin, is not seen as it really is.

It is filled with the intestines, the stomach, the lump of the liver, the abdomen, the heart, the lungs, the kidneys, the spleen,

With mucus, saliva, perspiration, lymph, blood, the fluid that lubricates the joints, bile, and fat.

Then in nine streams impurity flows always from it; from the eye the eye-excrement, from the ear the ear-excrement,

Mucus from the nose, through the mouth it ejects at one time bile and at other times it ejects phlegm, and from all the body come sweat and dirt.

Then its hollow head is filled with thc brain. A fool led by ignorance thinks it a fine thing.

And when it lies dead, swollen and livid, discarded in the cemetery, relatives do not care for it.

Dogs eat it and jackals, wolves and worms, crows and vultures eat it, and what other living creatures there are.

The Bhikkhu possessed of understanding in this world, having listened to Buddha's word, he certainly knows it, the body, thoroughly, for he sees it as it really is.

As this living body is, so is that dead one; as this is, so that will be; let one put away desire for the body, both as to its interior and as to its exterior.

Such a Bhikkhu who has turned away from desire and attachment, and is possessed of understanding in this world, has already gone to the immortal peace, the unchangeable state of Nibbana.

This body with two feet is cherished although impure, ill-smelling, filled with various kinds of stench, and trickling here and there.

He who with such a body thinks to exalt himself or despises others—what else is this but blindness?

12.

Houselife Defiling, Houseless Good

(Muni Sutta)

Definition of a Muni.

From acquaintanceship arises fear, from houselife arises defilement; the houseless state, freedom from acquaintanceship—this is indeed the view of a Muni.

Whosoever, after having uprooted his sin that has arisen, would not replant it and would not allow it to grow up again, him the solitarily wandering they call a Muni; such a great Isi has seen the state of peace.

Having considered the causes of sin, and having discerned the seed, let him not allow any desire for it to arise again, such a Muni who sees the end of birth and destruction, i.e., Nibbana, after leaving reasoning behind, does not enter the number of living beings.

He who has penetrated all the resting-places of the mind, and does not wish for any of them,—such a Muni indeed, free from covetousness and free from greediness, strives no longer, for he has reached the other shore.

The man who has overcome everything, who knows everything, who is possessed of good understanding, undefiled in all things, abandoning everything, liberated in the destruction of desire, i.e., Nibbana, him the wise style a Muni.

The man who has the strength of understanding, is endowed with virtue and holy works, is composed, delights in meditation, is thoughtful, free from ties, free from harshness and free from passion, him the wise style a Muni.

The Muni that wanders solitarily, the zealous, that is not shaken by blame and praise, like a lion not trembling at noises, like the wind not caught in a net, like a lotus not soiled by water, leading others, not led by others, him the wise style a Muni.

Whosoever becomes firm as the post in a bathing-place, in whom others acknowledge propriety of speech, who is free from passion, and endowed with well-composed senses, such a one the wise style a Muni.

Whosoever is firm, like a straight shuttle, and is disgusted with evil actions, reflecting on what is just and unjust, him the wise style a Muni.

Whosoever is self-restrained and does not do evil, is a young or middle-aged Muni, self-subdued, one that should not be provoked as he does not provoke any, him the wise style a Muni.

Whosoever, living upon what is given by others, receives a lump of rice from the top, from the middle or from the rest of the vessel, and does not praise the giver nor speak harsh words, him the wise style a Muni.

The Muni that wanders about abstaining from sexual intercourse, who in his youth is not fettered in any case, is abstaining from the insanity of pride, liberated, him the wise style a Muni.

The man who having penetrated the world, sees the highest truth, such a one, after crossing the stream and sea of existence, who has cut off all ties, is independent, free from passion, him indeed the wise style a Muni.

Two whose mode of life and occupation are quite different, are not equal: a householder maintaining a wife, and an unselfish virtuous man. A householder is intent upon the destruction of other living creatures, being unrestrained; but a Muni always protects living creatures, being restrained.

As the crested bird with the blue neck, the peacock never attains the swiftness of the swan, even so a householder does not equal a Bhikkhu, a secluded Muni meditating in the wood.

❖❖❖

Bodhisattva Avalokiteshwara, Cave 4

The Buddha of Light, at Nara, Japan.
53½ feet in height.

2
The Small Section
(Chulavagga)

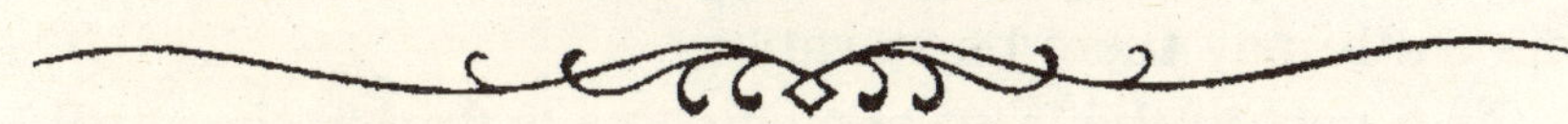

1.
Buddha, Dhamma, and Sangh
(Ratana Sutta)

For all beings salvation is only to be found in Buddha, Dhamma, and Sangh.

Whatever spirits have come together here, either belonging to the earth or living in the air, let all spirits be happy, and then listen attentively to what is said.

Therefore, O spirits, do ye all pay attention, show kindness to the human race who both day and night bring their offerings; therefore protect them strenuously.

Whatever wealth there be here or in the other world, or whatever excellent jewel in the heavens, it is certainly not equal to Tathagata. This excellent jewel is found in Buddha, by this truth may there be salvation.

The destruction of passion, the freedom from passion, the excellent immortality which Sakyamuni attained being composed,—there is nothing equal to that Dhamma. This excellent jewel is found in the Dhamma, by this truth may there be salvation.

The purity which be best of Buddhas praised, the meditation which they call uninterrupted, there is no meditation like this. This excellent jewel is found in the Dhamma, by this truth may there be salvation.

The eight persons that are praised by the righteous, and make these four pairs, they are worthy of offerings, being Sugata's disciple; what is given to these will bear great fruit. This excellent jewel is found in the Sangh, by this truth may there be salvation.

Those who have applied themselves studiously with a firm mind and free from desire to the commandments of Gotama, have obtained the highest gain, having merged into immortality, and enjoying happiness after getting it for nothing. This excellent jewel is found in the Sangh, by this truth may there be salvation.

As a post in the front of a city gate is firm in the earth and cannot be shaken by the four winds, like that I declare the righteous man to be who, having penetrated the noble truths, sees them clearly. This excellent jewel is found in the Sangh, by this truth may there be salvation.

Those who understand the noble truths well taught by the profoundly wise, i.e., Buddha, though they be greatly distracted, will not have to take the eighth birth. This excellent jewel is found in the Sangh, by this truth may there be salvation.

On his attaining the bliss of the right view three Dhammas are left behind by him: conceit and doubt and whatever he has got of virtue and holy works. He is released also from the four hells, and he is incapable of committing the six deadly sins. This excellent jewel is found in the Sangh, by this truth may there be salvation.

Even if he commits a sinful deed by his body, or in word or in thought, he is incapable of concealing it, for to conceal is said to be impossible for one that has seen the state of Nibbana. This excellent jewel is found in the Sangh, by this truth may there be salvation.

As in a clump of trees with their tops in bloom in the first heat of the hot month, so Buddha taught the excellent Dhamma leading to Nibbana to the greatest benefit for all. This excellent jewel is found in Buddha, by this truth may there be salvation.

The excellent one who knows what is excellent, who gives what is excellent, and who brings what is excellent, the incomparable one taught the excellent Dhamma. This excellent jewel is found in Buddha, by this truth may there be salvation.

The old is destroyed, the new has not arisen, those whose minds are disgusted with a future existence, the wise who have destroyed their seeds of existence, and whose desires do not increase, go out like this lamp. This excellent jewel is found in the Sangh, by this truth may there be salvation.

Whatever spirits have come together here, either belonging to the earth or living in the air, let us worship the perfect Buddha, revered by gods and men; may there be salvation.

Whatever spirits have come together here, either belonging to the earth or living in the air, let us worship the perfect Dhamma, revered by gods and men; may there be salvation.

Whatever spirits have come together here, either belonging to the earth or living in the air, let us worship the perfect Sangh, revered by gods and men; may there be salvation.

2.

Neither Flesh Nor Fasting, Nor Oblations

(Amagandha Sutta)

A bad mind and wicked deeds are what defiles a man; no outward observances can purify him.

Amagandha Brahmin: 'Those who eat Samaka, Chingulaka, and Chinaka, Pattaphala, Mulaphala, and Gaviphala (different sorts of grass, leaves, roots, etc.), justly obtained of the just, do not speak falsehood, nor are they desirous of sensual pleasures.

'He who eats what has been well prepared, well dressed, what is pure and excellent, given by others, he who enjoys food made of rice, eats, O Kassapa, what defiles one, i.e., Amagandha.

'The charge of Amagandha does not apply to me,' so thou say, 'O Brahmin (Brahmabandhu, although) enjoying food made of rice together with the well-prepared flesh of birds. I ask thee, O Kassapa, the meaning of this, of what description is then thy Amagandha?'

Kassapabuddha: 'Destroying living beings, killing, cutting, binding, stealing, speaking falsehood, fraud and deception, worthless reading, intercourse with another's wife;—this is Amagandha, but not eating of flesh.

'Those persons who in this world are unrestrained in enjoying sensual pleasures, greedy of sweet things, associated with what is impure, sceptics, unjust, difficult to follow;—this is Amagandha, but not the eating of flesh.

'Those who are rough, harsh, backbiting, treacherous, merciless, arrogant, and who being illiberal do not give anything to anyone;—this is Amagandha, but not the eating of flesh.

'Anger, intoxication, obstinacy, bigotry, deceit, envy, grandiloquence, pride and conceit, intimacy with the unjust;—this is Amagandha, but not the eating of flesh.

'Those who in this world are wicked, and such as do not pay their debts, are slanderers, false in their dealings, counterfeiters, those who in this world being the lowest of men commit sin;—this is Amagandha, but not the eating of flesh.

'Those persons who in this world are unrestrained in their behaviour towards living creatures, who are bent upon injuring after taking others' goods, wicked, cruel, harsh, disrespectful;—this is Amagandha, but not the eating of flesh.

'Those creatures who are greedy of these, living beings, who are hostile, offending; always bent upon evil, and therefore, when dead, go to darkness and fall with theIr heads downwards into hell;—this is Amagandha, but not the eating of flesh.

'Neither the flesh of fish, nor fasting, nor nakedness, nor tonsure, nor matted hair, nor dirt, nor rough skins, nor the worshipping of the fire, nor the many immortal penances in the world, nor hymns, nor oblations, nor sacrifice, nor observance of the seasons, purify a mortal who has not conquered his doubt.

'The wise man wanders about with his organs of sense guarded, and his senses conquered, standing firm in the Dhamma, delighting in what is right and mild; having overcome all ties and left behind all pain, he does not cling to what is seen and heard.'

Thus Bhagavat (Kassapa) preached this subject again and again, and the Brahmin who was accomplished in the hymns of the Vedas understood it; the Muni who is free from defilement, independent, and difficult to follow, made it clear in various stanzas.

Having heard the Buddha's well-spoken words, which are free from defilement and send away all pain, he worshipped the Tathagata's feet in humility, and took orders at once.

3.
A Good Friend Is He, Who . . .

(Hiri Sutta)

On true friendship.

He who transgresses and despises modesty, who says, 'I am a friend,' but does not undertake any work that can be done, know about him: 'he is not my friend.'

Whosoever uses pleasing words to friends without effect, him the wise know as one that only talks, but does not do anything.

He is not a friend who always eagerly suspects a breach and looks out for faults; but he with whom he dwells as a son at the breast of his mother, he is indeed a friend that cannot be severed from him by others.

He who hopes for fruit, cultivates the energy that produces joy and the pleasure that brings praise, while carrying the human yoke.

Having tasted the sweetness of seclusion and tranquillity one becomes free from fear and free from sin, drinking in the sweetness of the Dhamma.

4.

The Highest Blessings Are . . .

(Mahamangala Sutta)

Buddha defines the highest blessings to a deity.

So it was heard by me:

At one time Bhagavat dwelt at Savatthi, in Jetavana, in the park of Anathapindika. Then, when the night had come near, a deity of beautiful appearance, having illuminated the whole Jetavana, approached Bhagavat, and having approached and saluted him, he stood apart, and standing apart that deity addressed Bhagavat in a stanza:

'Many gods and men have devised blessings, longing for happiness, tell thou me the highest blessing.'

Buddha said: 'Not cultivating the society of fools, but cultivating the society of wise men, worshipping those that are to be worshipped, this is the highest blessing.

'To live in a suitable country, to have done good deeds in a former existence, and a thorough study of one's self, this is the highest blessing.

'Great learning and skill, well-learnt discipline, and well-spoken words, this is the highest blessing.

'Waiting on mother and father, protectmg child and wife, and a quiet calling, this is the highest blessing.

'Giving alms, living religiously, protecting relatives, blameless deeds, this is the highest blessing.

Bodhisattva Vajrapani, Cave 1

'Ceasing and abstaining from sin, refraining from intoxicating drink, perseverance in the Dhammas, this is the highest blessing.

'Reverence and humility, contentment and gratitude, the hearing of the Dhamma at due seasons, this is the highest blessing.

'Patience and pleasant speech, intercourse with Samanas, religious conversation at due seasons, this is the highest blessing.

'Penance and chastity, discernment of the noble truths, and the realisation of Nibbana, this is the highest blessing.

'He whose mind is not shaken when he is touched by the things of the world, Lokadhamma, but remains free from sorrow, free from defilement, and secure, this is the highest blessing.

'Those who, having done such things, are undefeated in every respect, walk in safety everywhere, theirs is the highest blessing.'

5.

Passion, Hatred, Disgust, Horror

(Suchiloma Sutta)

The Yakkha Suchiloma threatens to harm Buddha, if he cannot answer his questions. Buddha answers that all passions proceed from the body.

So it was heard by me:

At one time Bhagavat dwelt at Gaya, seated on a stone in the realm of the Yakkha Suchiloma. And at that time the Yakkha Khara and the Yakkha Suchiloma passed by, not far from Bhagavat. And then the Yakkha Khara said this to the Yakkha Suchiloma:'Is this man a Samana?'

Suchiloma answered: 'He is no Samana, he is a Samanaka, a wretched Samana; however, I will ascertain whether he is a Samana or a Samanaka.'

Then the Yakkha Suchiloma went up to Bhagavat, and having gone up to him, he brushed against Bhagavat's body. Then Bhagavat took away his body. Then the Yakkha Suchiloma said this to Bhagavat: 'O Samana, art thou afraid of me?'

Bhagavat answered: 'No, friend, I am not afraid of thee, but thy touching me is sinful.'

Suchiloma said: 'I will ask thee a question, O Samana; if thou canst not answer it I will either scatter thy thoughts or cleave thy heart, or take thee by the feet and throw thee over to the other shore of the Ganga.'

Bhagavat answered: 'I do not see, O friend, neither in this world together with the world of the Devas, Maras, Brahmins, nor, amongst the generation of Samana and Brahmins, gods and men, the one who can either scatter my thoughts or cleave my heart, or take me by the feet and throw me over to the other shore of the Ganga. However, ask, O friend, what thou pleasest.'

Then the Yakkha Suchiloma addressed Bhagavat in a stanza:

'What origin have passion and hatred, disgust, delight, and horror? wherefrom do they arise? whence arising do doubts vex the mind, as boys vex a crow?'

Buddha said: 'Passion and hatred have their origin from this body: disgust, delight, and horror arise from this body; arising from this body doubts vex the mind, as boys vex a crow.

'They originate in desire, they arise in self, like the shoots of the banyan tree; far and wide they are connected with sensual pleasures, like the Maluva creeper spread in the wood.

'Those who know whence a sin arises, drive it away. Listen, O Yakkha! they cross over this stream that is difficult to cross, and has not been crossed before, with a view to not being born again.'

6.

Be Pure and Live with the Pure

(Dhammachariya Sutta or Kapila Sutta)

The Bhikkhus are admonished to rid themselves of sinful persons, and advised to lead a pure life.

A just life, a religious life, this they call the best gem, if anyone has gone forth from houselife to a houseless life.

But if he be harsh-spoken, and like a beast delighting in injuring others, then the life of such a one is very wicked, and he increases his own pollution.

A Bhikkhu who delights in quarrelling and is shrouded in folly, does not understand the Dhamma that is preached and taught by Buddha.

Injuring his own cultivated mind, and led by ignorance, he does not understand that sin is the way leading to hell.

Having gone to calamity, from womb to womb, from darkness to darkness, such a Bhikkhu, verily, after passing away, goes to pain.

As when there is a pit of excrement that has become full during a number of years,—he who should be such a one full of sin is difficult to purify.

Whom you know to be such a one, O Bhikkhus, a man dependent on a house, having sinful desires, sinful thoughts, and being with sinful deeds and objects,

Him do avoid, being all in concord; blow him away as sweepings, put him away as rubbish.

Then remove as chaff those that are no Samanas, but only think themselves, blowing away those that have sinful desires and those with sinful deeds and objects.

Be pure and live together with the pure, being thoughtful; then agreeing and wise you will put an end to pain.

7.

The Brahmins Now-a-Days

(Brahminadhammika Sutta)

Wealthy Brahmins come to Buddha asking about the customs of the ancient Brahmins. Buddha descries their mode of life and the change wrought in them by seeing the king's riches, and furthermore, how they induced the king to commit the sin of having living creatures slain at sacrifices. On hearing Buddha's enlightened discourse the wealthy Brahmins are converted,

So it was heard by me:

At one time Bhagavat dwelt at Savatthi, in Jetavana in the park of Anathapindika. Then many wealthy Brahmins of Kosala, decrepit, elderly, old, advanced in age, or arrived at extreme old age, went to Bhagavat, and having gone to him they talked pleasantly with him, and after having had some pleasant and remarkable talk with him, they sat down apart. Sitting down apart these wealthy Brahmins said this to Bhagavat: 'O venerable Gotama, are the Brahmins now-a-days seen engaged in the Dhamma of the ancient Brahmins?'

Bhagavat answered: 'The Brahmins now-a-days, O Brahmins, are not seen engaged in, the customs of the ancient Brahmins.'

The Brahmins said: 'Let the venerable Gotama tell us the Brahminical customs of the ancient Brahmins, if it is not inconvenient to the venerable Gotama.'

Bhagavat answered: 'Then listen, O Brahmins, pay attention, I will speak.'

'Yes,' so saying the wealthy Brahmins listened to Bhagavat.

Bhagavat said this:

'The old sages were self-restrained, penitent; having abandoned the objects of the five senses, they studied their own welfare.

'There were no cattle for the Brahmins, nor gold, nor corn, but the riches and corn of meditation were for them, and they kept watch over the best treasure.

'What was prepared for them and placed as food at the door, they thought was to be given to those that seek for what has been prepared by faith.

'With garments variously coloured, with beds and abodes, prosperous people from the provinces and the whole country worshipped those Brahmins.

'Inviolable were the Brahmins, invincible, protected by the Dhamma, no one opposed them while standing at the doors of the houses anywhere.

'For forty-eight years they practised chastity, the Brahmins formerly went in search of knowledge and exemplary conduct.

'The Brahmins did not marry a woman belonging to another caste nor did they buy a wife; they chose living together in mutual love after having come together.

'Excepting from the time about the cessation of the menstruation else the Brahmins did not indulge in sexual intercourse.

'They praised chastity and virtue, rectitude, mildness, penance, tenderness, compassion, and patience.

'He who was the best of them, a strong Brahmin, did not even in sleep indulge in sexual intercourse.

'Imitating his practices some wise men in this world praised chastity, virtue, and patience.

'Having asked for rice, beds, garments, butter, and oil, and gathered them justly, they made sacrifices out of them, and when the sacrifice came on they did not kill cows.

'Like unto a mother, a father, a brother, and other relatives the cows are our best friends, in which medicines are produced.

'They give food, and they give strength, they likewise give a good complexion and happiness: knowing the real state of this, they did not kill cows.

'They were graceful, large, handsome, renowned, Brahmins by nature, zealous for their several works; as long as they lived in the world, this race prospered.

'But there was a change in them: after gradually seeing the king's prosperity and adorned women,

'Well-made chariots drawn by noble horses, carpets in variegated colours, palaces and houses, divided into compartments and measured out,

'The great human wealth, attended with a number of cows, and combined with a flock of beautiful women, the Brahmins became covetous.

'They then, in thls matter, having composed hymns, went to Okkaka, and said: "Thou hast much wealth and corn, sacrifice, for great is thy property, sacrifice, for great is thy wealth."

'And then the king, the lord of chariots, instructed by the Brahmins, brought about Passamedha, Purisamedha, Sammapasa, and Vachapeyya without any hinderance, and having offered these sacrifices, he gave the Brahmins wealth;

'Cows, beds, garments, and adorned women, and well-made chariots, drawn by noble horses, carpets in variegated colours,

'Beautiful palaces, well divided into compartments; and having filled these with different sorts of corn, he gave this wealth to the Brahmins.

'And they having thus received wealth wished for a store, and the craving of those who had given way to their wishes increased still more; they then in this matter, having composed hymns, went again to Okkaka, and said:

'As water, earth, gold, wealth, and corn, even so are there cows for men, for this is a requisite for living beings;

sacrifice, for great is thy property, sacrifice, for great is thy wealth.

'And then the king, the lord of chariots instructed by the Brahmins, caused many hundred thousand cows to be slain in offerings.

'Not with their feet, nor with their horns do the cows hurt any one in any way, being like goats tender and yielding vessels of milk —still seizing them by the horns the king caused them to be slain with a weapon.

'Then the gods, the forefathers, Inda, the Asuras, and the Rakkhasas cried out: "This is injustice," because of the weapon falling on the cows.

'There were formerly three diseases: desire, hunger, and decay, but from the slaying of cattle there came ninety-eight.

'This injustice of using violence that has come down to us, was old; innocent cows are slain, the sacrificing priests have fallen off from the Dhamma.

'So this old and mean Dhamma is blamed by the wise; where people see such a one, they blame the sacrificing priest.

'So Dhamma being lost, the Suddas and the Vessikas disagreed, the Khattiyas disagreed in manifold ways, the wife despised her husband.

'The Khattiyas and the Brahmins and those others who had been protected by their castes after doing away with their disputes on descent, fell into power of sensual pleasures.'

This having been said, those wealty Brahmins said to Bhagavat as follows:

'It is excellent, O venerable Gotama! It is excellent, O venerable Gotama! As one raises what has been overthrown, or reveals what has been hidden, or tells the way to him who has gone astray, or holds out an oil lamp

Cave 26

in the dark that those who have eyes may see the objects, even so by the venerable Gotama in manifold ways the Dhamma has been illustrated; we take refuge in the venerable Gotama, in the Dhamma, and in the Sangh of Bhikkhus; may the venerable Gotama receive us as followers, who from this day for life have taken refuge in him.'

8.

Cultivate Good, Learned Men

(Nava Sutta)

On choosing a good and learned teacher.

A man should worship him from whom he learns the Dhamma, as the gods worship Inda; the learned man being worshipped and pleased with him, makes the highest Dhamma manifest.

Having heard and considered that the wise man practising the Dhamma that is in accordance with the highest Dhamma, becomes learned, expert, and skilful, strenuously associating with such a learned teacher.

He who serves a low teacher, a fool who has not understood the meaning, and who is envious, goes to death, not having overcome doubt, and not having understood the Dhamma.

As a man, after descending into a river, a turgid water with a rapid current, is borne along following the current, —how will he be able to put others across?

Even so how will a man, not having understood the Dhamma, and not attending to the explanation of the learned and not knowing it himself, not having overcome doubt, be able to make others understand it?

As one, having gone on board a strong ship, provided with oars and rudder, carries across in it many others, knowing the way to do it, and being expert and thoughtful,

So also he who is accomplished, of a cultivated mind, learned, intrepid, makes others endowed with attention and assiduity understand it, knowing it himself.

Therefore indeed one should cultivate the society of a good man, who is intelligent and learned; he who leads a regular life, having understood what is good and penetrated the Dhamma, will obtain happiness.

9.
Let Your Pleasure-Garden Be Dhamma
(Kimsila Sutta)

How to obtain the highest good.

By what virtue, by what conduct, and performing what works, will a man be perfectly established in the commandments and obtain the highest good?

Let him honour old people, not be envious, let him know the right time for seeing his teacher, and knowing the right moment let him assiduously listen to his religious discourses pronounced and to his well-spoken words.

Let him in due time go to the presence of his teacher, let him be humble after casting away obstinacy, let him remember and practise what is good, the Dhamma, self-restraint, and chastity.

Let his pleasure-garden be the Dhamma, let him delight in the Dhamma, let him stand fast in the Dhamma, let him know how to enquire into the Dhamma, let him not raise any dispute that pollutes the Dhamma, and let him spend his time in speaking well-spoken truths.

Having abandoned ridiculous talk, lamentation, corruption, deceit, hypocrisy, greediness and haughtiness, clamour and harshness, depravity and foolishness, let him live free from infatuation, with a steady mind.

The words, the essence of which is understood, are well spoken, and what is heard, if understood, contains the essence of meditation; but the understanding and learning of the man who is hasty and careless, does not increase.

Those who delight in the Dhamma, proclaimed by the venerable ones, are unsurpassed in speech, mind and work, they are established in peace, tenderness and meditation, and have gone to the essence of learning and understanding.

10.
Rise, Sit Up and Act
(Uttahana Sutta)

Advice not to be lukewarm and slothful.

Rise, sit up, what is the use of your sleeping; to those who are sick, pierced by the arrow of pain and suffering, what sleep is there?

Rise, sit up, learn steadfastly for the sake of peace, let not the king of death, knowing you to be indolent, befool you and lead you into his power.

Conquer this desire which gods and men stand wishing for and are dependent upon, let not the right moment pass by you; for those who have let the right moment pass, will grieve when they have been consigned to hell.

Indolence is defilement, continued indolence is defilement; by earnestness and knowledge let one pull out his arrow of passion.

11.
'Rahula, Sacrifice Your Pride and Wander Calm'
(Rahula Sutta)

Buddha recommends the life of a recluse to Rahula, and admonishes him to turn his mind away from the world and to be moderate.

Bhagavat said: 'Dost thou not despise the wise man, from living with him constantly? Is he who holds up a torch to mankind honoured by thee?'

Celestials in the Sky. Cave 17

Rahula: 'I do not despise the wise man, from living with him constantly; he who holds up a torch to mankind is always honoured by me.'

Bhagavat: 'Having abandoned the objects of the five senses, the beautiful, the charming, and gone out from thy house with faith, do thou put an end to pain?

'Cultivate the society of virtuous friends and a distant dwelling-place, secluded and quiet; be moderate in food.

'Robes, alms in bowl, requisites for the sick, a dwelling-place,—do not thirst after these things, that thou mayest not go back to the world again.

'Be subdued according to the precepts, and as to the five senses, be attentive as regards thy body, and be full of disgust with the world.

'Avoid signs, what is pleasant and is accompanied with passion, turn thy mind undisturbed and well composed to what is not pleasant.

'Cherish what is signless, leave the inclinations for pride; then by sacrificing thy pride thou shalt wander calm.'

So Bhagavat repeatedly admonished the venerable Rahula with these stanzas.

12.

He Crossed Birth and Death

(Vangisa Sutta)

Vangisa desires to know the fate of Nigrodhakappa, whether he has been completely extinguished, or whether he is still with some elements of existence left behind. He is answered by Buddha.

So it was heard by me:

At one time Bhagavat dwelt at Alavi, in the temple of Aggalava. At that time the teacher of the venerable Vangisa, the Thera, by name Nigrodhakappa, had attained bliss not long before. Then this reflection occurred to the venerable Vangisa, while retired and meditating:

Whether my teacher be blessed or whether he be not blessed. Then the venerable Vangisa, at the evening time, coming forth from his retirement went to Bhagavat, and having gone to him he sat down apart after saluting him, and sitting down apart the venerable Vangisa said this to Bhagavat:

'Lord, while retired and meditating, this reflection occurred to me here: Whether my teacher be blessed or whether he be not blessed.'

Then the venerable Vangisa, rising from his seat, throwing his robe over one shoulder and bending his joined hands towards Bhagavat, addressed him in stanzas:

'We ask the Master of excellent understanding: he who in this world had cut off doubt, died at Aggalava, a Bhikkhu, well known, famous, and of a calm mind.

'The name "Nigrodhakappa" was given to that Brahmin by thee, O Bhagavat; he wandered about worshipping thee, having liberation in view, strong, O thou who seest Nibbana.

'O Sakka, thou all-seeing, we all wish to learn something about this disciple; our ears are ready to hear, thou art our Master, thou art incomparable.

'Cut off our doubt, tell me of him, inform us of the blessed, O thou of great understanding; speak in the midst of us, O thou all-seeing, as the thousand-eyed Sakka speaks in the midst of the gods.

'Whatever ties there are in this world constituting the way to folly, combined with ignorance, forming the seat of doubt, they do not exist before Tathagata, for he is the best eye of men.

'If a man does not for ever dispel the sin as the wind dispels a mass of clouds, all the world will be enveloped in darkness, not even illustrious men will shine.

'Wise men are light-bringers, therefore, O wise man, I consider thee as such a one; we have come to him who beholds meditation, reveal Kappa to us in the Sangh.

'Uplift quickly, O thou beautiful one, thy beautiful voice, like the swans drawing up their necks, sing softly with a rich and well-modulated voice; we will all listen to thee attentively.

'Having earnestly called upon him who has completely left birth and death behind and shaken off sin, I will make him proclaim the Dhamma, for ordinary people cannot do what they want, but the Tathagatas act with a purpose.

'This full explanation by thee, the perfectly wise, is accepted, this last clasping of the hands is well bent, O thou of high wisdom, knowing Kappa's transmigration do not delude us.

'Having perfectly comprehended the Dhamma of the venerable ones, do not delude us, O thou of unsurpassed strength, knowing everything; as one the hot season pained by the heat longs for water, so I long for thy words; send a shower of learning.

'The rich religious life which Kappayana led has not that been in vain to him, has he been completely extinguished, or is he still with some elements of existence left behind? How he was liberated, that we want to hear.'

'He cut off the craving for name and form in this world,'—so said Bhagavat,—'Kanha's Mara's stream, adhered to for a long time, he crossed completely birth and death,' so said Bhagavat, the best of the five Brahmins, Panchavaggiya.

Vangisa: 'Having heard thy word, O thou the best of the Isis, I am pleased; not in vain have I asked, the Brahmin did not deceive me.

'As he talked so he acted, he was a true disciple of Buddha, he cut asunder the outspread strong net of deceitful death.

'Kappayana saw, O Bhagavat, the beginning of attachment, Kappayana verily crossed the realm of death, which is very difficult to cross.'

13.

Who Wanders Rightly in the World

(Sammaparibbajaniya Sutta)

The right path for a Bhikkhu.

'We will ask the Muni of great understanding, who has crossed, gone to the other shore, is blessed and of a firm mind: How does a Bhikkhu wander rightly in the world, after having gone out of his house and driven away desire?

'He whose ideas of omens, meteors, dreams and signs are destroyed,'—so said Bhagavat,—'such a Bhikkhu who has abandoned the sinful omens, wanders rightly in the world.

'Let the Bhikkhu subdue his passion for human and divine pleasures, then after conquering existence and understanding the Dhamma, such a one will wander rightly in the world.

'Let the Bhikkhu, after casting behind him slander and anger, abandon avarice and be free from compliance and opposition, then such a one will wander rightly in the world.

'He who having left behind both what is agreeable and what is disagreeable, not seizing upon anything, is independent in every respect and liberated from bonds, such a one will wander rightly in the world.

'He who does not see any essence in the Upadhis, having subdued his wish and passion for attachments, he is independent and not to be led by others, such a one will wander rightly in the world.

'He who is not opposed to any one in word, thought or deed, who after having understood the Dhamma perfectly, longs for the state of Nibbana, such a one will wander rightly in the world.

'He who thinking "he salutes me" is not elated, the Bhikkhu who, although abused, does not reflect upon it, and having received food from others does not get intoxicated with pride, such a one will wander rightly in the world.

'The Bhikkhu who, after leaving behind covetousness and existence, is disgusted with cutting and binding others, he who has overcome doubt, and is without pain, such a one will wander rightly in the world.

'And knowing what becomes him, the Bhikkhu will not harm anyone in the world, understanding the Dhamma thoroughly, such a one will wander rightly in the world.

'He to whom there are no affections whatsoever, whose sins are extirpated from the root, he free from desire and not longing for anything, such a one will wander rightly in the world.

'He whose passions have been destroyed, who is free from pride, who has overcome all the path of passion, is subdued, perfectly happy and of a firm mind, such a one will wander rightly in the world.

'The believer, possessed of knowledge, seeing the way leading to Nibbana, who is no partisan amongst the partisans of the sixty-two philosophical views, wise after subduing covetousness, hatred, such a one will wander rightly in the world.

He who is pure and victorious, who has reomoved the veil of the world, who is subdued in the Dhammas, has gone to the other shore, is without desire, and skilled in the knowledge of the cessation of the Samkharas, such a one will wander rightly in the world.

He who has overcome time in the past and in the future, is of an exceedingly pure understanding, liberated from all the dwelling-places of the mind, such a one will wander rightly in the world.

'Knowing the step of the four truths, understanding the Dhamma, seeing clearly the abandonment of the passions from the destruction of all the elements of existence, such a one will wander rightly in the world.'

'Certainly, O Bhagavat, it is so: whichever Bhikkhu lives in this way, subdued and having overcome all bonds, such a one will wander rightly in the world.'

14.

This Subtle and Pleasant Dhamma

(Dhammika Sutta)

Buddha shows Dhammika what the life of a Bhikkhu and what the life of a householder ought to be.

So it was heard by me:

At one time Bhagavat dwelt at Savatthi, in Jetavana, in the park of Anathapindika. Then the follower Dhammika, together with five hundred followers, went to Bhagavat, and having gone to Bhagavat and saluted him, he sat down apart; sitting down apart the follower Dhammika addressed Bhagavat in stanzas:

'I ask thee, O Gotama of great understanding, how is a Savaka disciple to act to be a good one? is it the one what goes from his house to the wilderness, or the followers with a house?

'For thou knowest the doings of this world and that of the gods, and the final end; there is nobody like thee seeing the subtle meaning of things; they call thee the excellent Buddha.

'Knowing all knowledge thou hast revealed the Dhamma, having compassion on creatures; thou hast removed the veil of the world, thou art all seeing, thou shinest spotless in all the world.

'The king of elephants, Eravalla by name, hearing that thou were Jina the Conqueror, came to thy presence, and having conversed with thee he went away delighted, after listening to thee and saying, "Very good!"

'Also king Vessavana Kuvera came to ask thee about the Dhamma; him, too, thou, O wise man, answered when asked, and he also after listening was delighted.

'All these disputatious Titthiyas and Ajivikas and Niganthas do not any of them overcome thee in understanding, as a man standing does not overcome the one that is walking quickly.

'All these disputatious Brahmins, and there are even some old Brahmins, all are bound by thy opinion, and others also that are considered disputants.

'This subtle and pleasant Dhamma that has been well proclaimed by thee, O Bhagavat, and which we all long to hear, do thou, O thou best of Buddhas, speak to us when asked.

'Let all these Bhikkhus and also Upasakas that have sat down to listen, hear the Dhamma learnt by the stainless Buddha, as the gods hear the well-spoken words of Vasava.'

Bhagavat: 'Listen to me, O Bhikkhus, I will teach you the Dhamma that destroys sin, do you keep it, all of you;

Lord Buddha, Pagan, Myanmar

let him who looks for what is salutary, the thoughtful, cultivate the mode of life suitable for Pabbajitas.

'Let not the Bhikkhu walk about at a wrong time, let him go to the village for alms at the right time; for ties ensnare the one that goes at a wrong time, therefore Buddhas do not go at a wrong time.

'Form, sound, taste, smell, and touch which intoxicate creatures, having subdued the desire for all these things, let him in due time go in for his breakfast.

'And let the Bhikkhu, alter having obtained his food at the right time and returned, sit down alone and privately; reflecting within himself, let him not turn his mind to outward things, but be self-collected.

'If he speak with a Savaka or with anybody else, or with a Bhikkhu, let him talk about the excellent Dhamma, but let him not utter slander, nor blaming words against others.

'For some utter language contradicting others; those narrow-minded ones we do not praise. Ties from here and there ensnare them, and they send their mind far away in that dispute.

'Let a Savaka of him with the excellent understanding, after hearing the Dhamma taught by Sugata, discriminately seek for food, a monastery, a bed and a chair, and water for taking away the dirt of his clothes.

'But without clinging to these things, to food, to bed and chair, to water for taking away the dirt of his clothes, let a Bhikkhu be like a waterdrop on a lotus.

'A householder's work I will also tell you, how a Savaka is to act to be a good one; for that complete Bhikkhu Dhamma cannot be carried out by one who is taken up by worldly occupations.

'Let him not kill, nor cause to be killed any living being, nor let him approve of others killing, after having refrained from hurting all creatures, both those that are strong and those that tremble in the world.

'Then let the Savaka abstain from taking anything from any place that has not been given to him, knowing it to belong to another, let him not cause anyone to take, nor approve of those that take, let him avoid all sort of theft.

'Let the wise man avoid an unchaste life as a burning heap of coals; not being able to live a life of chastity, let him not transgress with another man's wife.

'Let no one speak falsely to another in the hall of justice or in the hall of the Sangh, let him not cause any one to speak falsely nor approve of those that speak falsely, let him avoid all sort of untruth.

'Let the householder who approves of this Dhamma, not give himself to intoxicating drinks; let him not cause others to drink, nor approve of those that drink, knowing it to end in madness.

'For through intoxication the stupid commit sins and make other people intoxicated; let him avoid this seat of sin, this madness, this folly, delightful to the stupid.

'Let him not kill any living being, let him not take what has not been given to him, let him not speak falsely, and let him not drink intoxicating drinks, let him refrain from unchaste sexual intercourse, and let him not at night eat untimely food.

'Let him not wear wreaths nor use perfumes, let him lie on a couch spread on the earth:—this they call the eightfold abstinence, Uposatha, proclaimed by Buddha, who has overcome pain.

'Then having with a believing mind kept abstinence on the fourteenth, fifteenth, and the eighth days of the half-month, and having kept the complete Patiharak-apakkha consisting of eight parts,

'And then in the morning, after having kept abstinence, let a wise man with a believing mind, gladdening the Sangh of Bhikkhus with food and drink, make distributions according to his ability.

'Let him dutifully maintain his parents, and practise an honourable trade; the householder who observes this strenuously goes to the gods by name Sayampabhas.'

❖❖❖

Buddhist Sculpture from the Bharhut Stupe

3

The Large Section

(Mahavagga)

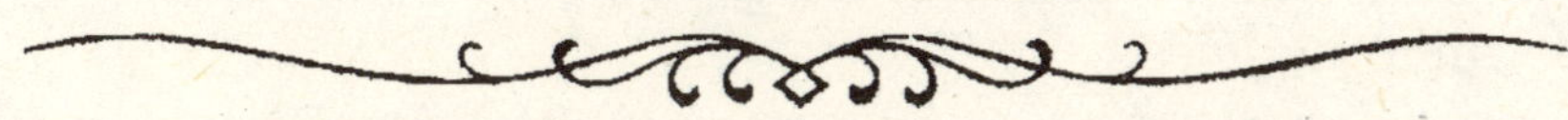

1.
Where Is the Bhikkhu Going?
(Pabbajja Sutta)

King Bimbisara, feeling interested in Buddha, tries to tempt him with wealth, but is mildly rebuked by him.

I will praise an ascetic life such as the clearly-seeing Buddha led, such as he thinking over it approved of as an ascetic life.

'This house-life is pain, the seat of impurity,' and 'an ascetic life is an open-air life,' so considering he embraced an ascetic life.

Leading an ascetic life, he avoided with his body sinful deeds, and having also abandoned sin in words, he cleansed his life.

Buddha went to Rajagaha, he entered the Giribbaja in Magadha for alms with a profusion of excellent signs.

Bimbisara standing in his palace saw him, and seeing him endowed with these signs, he spoke these words:

'Attend ye to this man, he is handsome, great, clean, he is both endowed with good conduct, and he does not look before him further than a yuga, the distance of a.plough.

With downcast eyes, thoughtful, this one is not like those of low caste; let the king's messengers run off, and ask; 'Where is the Bhikkhu going?'

The king's messengers followed after him, and said' 'Where is the Bhikkhu going, where will he reside?'

'Going begging from house to house, watching the door of the senses, well restrained, he quickly filled his bowl, conscious, thoughtful.

'Wandering about in search of alms, having one out of town, the Muni repaired to the mountain Pandava; it must be there he lives.'

Seeing that he had entered his dwelling, the messengers then sat down, and one messenger having returned announced it to the king:

'This Bhikkhu, O great king, is sitting on the east side of Pandava, like a tiger, like a bull, like a lion in a mountain cave.'

Having heard the messenger's words, the Khattiya in a fine chariot hastening went out to the Pandava mountain.

Having gone as far as the ground was practicable for a chariot, the Khattiya, after alighting from the chariot, and approaching on foot, having come up to him, seated himself.

Having sat down the king then exchanged the usual ceremonious greetings with him, and after the complimentary talk he spoke these words:

'Thou art both young and delicate, a lad in his first youth, possessed of a fine complexion, like a high-born Khattiya.

'I will ornament the army-house, and at the head of the assembly of chiefs give thee wealth; enjoy it and tell me thy birth, when asked.'

Buddha: 'Just beside Himavanta, O king, there live a people endowed with the power of wealth, the inhabitants of Kosala.

'They are Adichchas by family, Sakiyas by birth; from that family I have wandered out, not longing for sensual pleasures.

'Seeing misery in sensual pleasures, and considering the forsaking of the world as happiness, I will go and exert myself; in this my mind delights.'

2.

While the Flesh Is Wasting Away

(Padhana Sutta)

Mara tries to tempt Buddha, but disappointed, is obliged to withdraw.

To me, whose mind was intent upon exertion near the river Neranjara, having exerted myself, and given myself to meditation for the sake of acquiring Nibbana.

Came Namuchi speaking words full of compassion: 'Thou art lean, ill-favoured, death is in thy neighbourhood.

'A thousandth part of thee is the property of death, only one part belongs to life; living life, O thou venerable one, is better; living thou wilt be able to do good works.

'When thou livest a religious life, and feedest the sacrificial fire, manifold good works are woven to thee; what dost thou want with exertion?

'Difficult is the way of exertion, difficult to pass, difficult to enter upon;' saying these verses Mara stood near Buddha.

To Mara thus speaking Bhagavat said this: 'O thou friend of indolent, thou wicked one, for what purpose hast thou come here?

'Even the least good work is of no use to me; and what good works are required, Mara ought to tell.

'I have faith and power, and understanding is found in me; while thus exerting myself, why do you ask me to live?

'This burning wind will dry up even the currents of the rivers; should it not by degrees dry up my blood, while I am exerting myself?

'While the blood is drying up, the bile and the phlegm are dried up; while the flesh is wasting away, the mind gets more tranquil, and my attention, understanding, and meditation get more steadfast.

'While I am living thus, after having felt the extreme sensations, my mind does not look for sensual pleasures; behold a being's purity.

'Lust thy first army is called, discontent thy second, thy third is called hunger and thirst, thy fourth craving.

'Thy fifth is called sloth and drowsiness, thy sixth cowardice, thy seventh doubt, thy eighth hypocrisy and stupor,

'Gain, fame, honour, and what celebrity has been falsely obtained; and he who exalts himself and despises others.

'This, O Namuchi, is thine, the black one's fighting army; none but a hero conquers it, and after conquering it obtains joy.

'I myself having conquered wear Munja grass. Woe upon life in this world! death in battle is better for me than that I should live defeated.

'Plunged into this world some Samanas and Brahmins are not seen, and they do not know the way in which the virtuous walk.

'Seeing on all sides an army arrayed, and Mara on his elephant, I am going out to do battle, that he may not drive me away from my place.

'This army of thine, which the world of men and gods cannot conquer, I will crush with understanding as one crushes an unbaked earthen pot with a stone.

'Having made my thought subject to me and my attention firm, I shall wander about from kingdom to kingdom, training disciples extensively.

'They will be zealous and energetic, executing my orders, the orders of one free from lust, and they will go to the place where, having gone, they will not mourn.'

Mara: 'For seven years I followed Bhagavat step by step; I found no fault in the perfectly enlightened, thoughtful Buddha.

'The crow hovered round the rock that looked like a lump of fat: "Do we here find something soft, is it something sweet?"

'Having obtained nothing sweet there, the crow went away from that spot. Thus like the crow approaching the rock, being disgusted, we shall go away from Gotama.'

While overcome with sorrow the string of his lute slipped down; then that evil-minded Yakkha disappeared there.

3.

Speak What Is Right, Pleasing and True
(Subhasita Sutta)

On well-spoken Language.

So it was heard by me:

At one time Bhagavat dwelt at Savatthi in Jetavana. Bhagavat said this: 'O Bhikkhus, the speech that is provided with four requisites is well-spoken, not ill-spoken, both faultless and blameless to the wise.'

'Which four?'

'O Bhikkhus, the Bhikkhu speaks well-spoken language, not ill-spoken; he speaks what is right (Dhamma) not what is unrighteous (Adhamma); he speaks what is pleasing, not what is unpleasing; he speaks what is true, not what is false. O Bhikkhus, the speech that is provided with these four requisites, is well-spoken, not ill-spoken, both faultless and blameless to the wise.'

This said Bhagavat. When Sugata had said this, then the Master spoke the following:

'Well-spoken language, the first, call the principal thing; let one speak what is right not what is unrighteous, that is that second; let one speak what is pleasing, not what is unpleasing, that is the third; let one speak what is true, not what is false, that is the fourth.'

Then the venerable Vangisa, rising from his seat, throwing his robe over one shoulder and bending his joined hands towards Bhagavat, said this: 'It occurs to me, O Sugata!'

'Let it occur to thee, O Vangisa!' said Bhagavat.

Then the venerable Vangisa, standing before Bhagavat, praised him with appropriate stanzas:

'Let one say such words by which he does not pain himself, nor hurt others; such words are truly well-spoken.

'Let one speak pleasing words which are received joyfully by all, and which saying he, without committing sins, speaks what is pleasing to others.

'Truth verily is immortal speech, this is a true saying; in what is true, in what is good, and in what is right, the just stand firm, so they say.

'The words which Buddha speaks, which are sure to bring about extinction and put an end to pain, such words are truly the best.'

4.

Who Deserves the Oblation?

(Sundarikabharadvaja Sutta)

Buddha shows to Sundarikabharadvaja on whom to bestow oblations, and the Brahmin is finally converted.

So it was heard by me:

At one time Bhagavat dwelt in Kosala on the bank of the river Sundarika. And during that time the Brahmin Sundarikabharadvaja made offerings to the fire and worshipped the fire. Then the Brahmin Sundarikabharadvaja, having made offerings to the fire

Attacks of Mara. Cave 1

and worshipped the fire, and having risen from his seat, looked about him on all sides towards the four quarters of the globe, saying: 'Who is to enjoy the rest of this oblation?'

The Brahmin Sundarikabharadvaja saw Bhagavat sitting not far off at the root of a tree, wrapped up head and body; and seeing him he, after taking the rest of the oblation with his left hand and the waterpot with his right hand, went up to Bhagavat. Then Bhagavat, on hearing the footsteps of Sundarikabharadvaja, the Brahmin, uncovered his head.

Then the Brahmin Sundarikabharadvaja thought: 'This man is shaved, this man is a shaveling,' and he wished to return again from there. Then this came to the mind of Sundarikabharadvaja, the Brahmin: 'Some Brahmins also here are shaved, I think I shall go up and ask him about his descent.' Then the Brahmin Sundarikabharadvaja went up to Bhagavat, and having gone up he said this: 'Of what family art thou?'

Then Bhagavat answered Sundarikabharadvaja the Brahmin, in stanzas:

'No Brahmin am I, nor a king's son, nor any Vessa; having thoroughly observed the class of common people, I wander about the world reflectingly, possessing nothing.

'Dressed in a *sanghati* and houseless I wander about, with my hair cut off, calm, not intermixing with people in this world. Thou askest me an unreasonable question about my family, O Brahmin.'

Sundarikabharadvaja: 'Sir, Brahmins together with Brahmins ask truly, Art thou a Brahmin?'

Bhagavat: 'If thou sayest I am a Brahmin and callest me no Brahmin, then I ask thee about the Savitti that consists of three padas and twentyfour syllables.'

Sundarikabharadvaja: 'For what reason did the Isis, men, Khattiyas, Brahmins make offerings to the gods abundantly in this world?'

Bhagavat: 'He who, perfect and accomplished at the time of offering, obtains the ear of one or the other god, he will succeed, so I say.'

'Surely his offering will bear fruit,'—so said the Brahmin,—'because we saw such an accomplished man; for by not seeing such as you, somebody else will enjoy the oblation.'

Bhagavat: 'Therefore, O Brahmin, as you have come here to ask for something, ask; perhaps thou mightest here find one that is calm, without anger, free from pain, free from desire, one with a good understanding.'

Sundarikabharadvaja: 'I delight in offering, O Gotama, I desire to make an offering, but I do not understand it; do thou instruct me, tell me in what case the offerig succeeds.'

Bhagavat: 'Therefore, O Brahmin, lend me thy ear, I will teach thee the Dhamma.

'Do not ask about descent, but ask about conduct; from wood, it is true, fire is born; likewise a firm Muni, although belonging to a low family, may become noble, when restrained from sinning by humility.

'He who is subdued by truth, endowed with temperance, accomplished, leading a religious life, on such a one in due time people should bestow oblations; let the Brahmin who has good works in view, offer.

'Those who, after leaving sensual pleasures, wander about houseless, well restrained, being like a straight shuttle, on such in due time people should bestow oblations; let the Brahmin who has good works in view, offer.

'Those whose passions are gone, whose senses are well composed, who are liberated like the moon out of the grasp of Rahu, on such in due time people should bestow oblations; let the Brahmin who has good works in view, offer.

'Those who wander about in the world without clinging to anything, always thoughtful, having left selfishness, on such in due time people should bestow oblations; let the Brahmin who has good works in view, offer.

'He who, after leaving sensual pleasures, wanders about victorious, he who knows the end of birth and death, who is perfectly happy, calm like deep water, Tathagata deserves the oblation.

'Just with the just and far from the unjust, Tathagata is possessed of infinite understanding: undefiled both in this world and in the other, Tathagata deserves the oblation.

'He in whom there lives no deceit, no arrogance, he who is free from cupidity, free from selfishness, free from desire, who has banished anger, who is calm, the Brahmin who has removed the taint of grief, Tathagata deserves the oblation.

'He who has banished every resting-place of the mind, he for whom there is no grasping, he who covets nothing either in this world or in the other, Tathagata deserves the oblation.

'He who is composed, who has crossed over the stream of existence and knows the Dhamma by taking the highest view of it, he whose passions are destroyed, who is wearing the last body, Tathagata deserves the oblation.

'He whose passion for existence and whose harsh talk are destroyed, are perished, and therefore exist not, he the accomplished and in every respect liberated Tathagata deserves the oblation.

'He who has shaken off all ties, for whom there are no ties, who amongst arrogant beings is free from arrogance, having penetrated pain together with its domain and subject, Tathagata deserves the oblation.

'He who, without giving himself up to desire, sees Nibbana, who has overcome the view that is to be taught by others, to whom there are no objects of sense whatever, Tathagata deserves the oblation.

'He to whom all Dhammas of every description, after he has penetrated them, are destroyed, are perished, and therefore exist not, he who is calm, liberated in the destruction of attachment, Tathagata deserves the oblation.

'He who sees the destruction of bond and birth, who has totally evaded the path of passion, who is pure, faultless, spotless, undepraved, Tathagata deserves the oblation.

'He who does not measure himself by himself, who is composed, upright, firm, without desire, free from harshness, free from doubt, Tathagata deserves the oblation.

'He to whom there is no cause of folly, who has a supernatural insight in all Dhammas, who wears the last body, and who has acquired perfect enlightenment, the highest, the blessed, for him thus a Yakkha's purification takes place.'

Sundarikabharadvaja: 'May my offering be a true offering, because I met with such an accomplished one; Brahmin is my witness, may Bhagavat accept me, may Bhagavat enjoy my oblation.'

Bhagavat: 'What is obtained by stanzas is not to be enjoyed by me, this is not the custom of the clearly-seeing, O Brahmin; Buddhas reject what is obtained by stanzas. While the Dhamma exists, O Brahmin, this is the practice of the Buddha.

'With other food and drink must thou serve one that is perfect, a great Isi, whose passions are destroyed, and whose misbehaviour has ceased, for this is a field for one who looks for good works.'

Sundarikabharadvaja: 'Good, O Bhagavat, then I should like to know, who will enjoy a gift from one like me, and whom I shall seek at the time of sacrifice as one worthy of offerings after having accepted thy doctrine.'

Bhagavat: 'Whosoever has no quarrels, whose mind is untroubled, and who has freed himself from lusts, whose sloth is driven away,

'Whosoever conquers his sins, knows birth and death, the Muni who is endowed with wisdom, such a one who has attained to offering,

'Him you should worship and honour with food and drink, putting away frowning; so the gifts will prosper;'

Sundarikabharadvaja: 'Thou Buddha deservest the oblation, thou art the best field for good works, the object of offering to all the world; what is given to thee will bear great fruit.'

Then the Brahmin Sundarikabharadvaja said this to Bhagavat: 'It is excellent, O venerable Gotama! It is excellent, O venerable Gotama! As one raises what has been overthrown, or reveals what has been hidden, or tells the way to him who has gone astray, or holds out an oil lamp in the dark that those who have eyes may see the objects, even so by the venerable Gotama in manifold ways the Dhamma has been illustrated; I take refuge in the venerable Gotama, in the Dhamma, and in the Sangh of Bhikkhus; I wish to receive the robe and the orders from the venerable Gotama.'

The Brahmin Sundarikabharadvaja received the Pabbajja from Bhagavat, and he received also the Upasampada; and the venerable Bharadvaja, having lately received the Upasampada, leading a solitary, retired, strenuous, ardent, energetic life, lived after having in a short time in this existence by his own understanding ascertained and possessed himself of that highest perfection of a religious life for the sake of which men of good family rightly wander away from their houses to a houseless state. 'Birth had been destroyed, a religious life had been led, what was to be done had been done, there was nothing else to be done for this existence,' so he perceived, and the venerable Bharadvaja became one of the arahats.

5.
Who Is Worthy of Offerings?
(Magha Sutta)

Buddha on being asked tells Magha of those worthy of offerings and the blessing of offerings.

So it was heard by me:

At one time Bhagavat dwelt at Rajagaha, in the mountain called the Gijjhakuta.

Then the young man Magha went to Bhagavat, and having gone to him he talked pleasantly with him, and after having had some pleasant, remarkable conversation with him he sat down apart; sitting down apart the young man Magha spoke this to Bhagavat:

'O venerable Gotama, I am a liberal giver, bountiful, suitable to beg of; justly I seek for riches, and having sought for riches justly, I give out of the justly obtained and justly acquired riches to one, to two, to three, to four, to five, to six, to seven, to eight, to nine, to ten, to twenty, to thirty, .to forty, to fifty, to a hundred, I give still more. I should like to know, O venerable Gotama, whether I, while so giving, so offering, produce much good.'

'Certainly, O young man, dost thou in so offering produce much good; he, O young man, who is a liberal giver, bountiful, suitable to beg of, and who justly seeks for riches, and having sought for riches justly, gives out of his justly obtained and justly acquired riches to one, to two, to three, to four, to five, to six, to seven, to eight, to nine, to ten, to twenty, to thirty, to forty, to fifty, to a hundred, and gives still more, produces much good.'

Then the young man Magha addressed Bhagavat in stanzas:

'I ask the venerable Gotama, the bountiful,'—so said the young man Magha,—'wearing the yellow robe, wandering about houseless: He who is a householder, suitable to beg of, a donor, who, desirous of good, offers having what is good in view, and giving to others in this world food and drink,—where, on whom bestowed will the oblation of such an offerer prosper?'

'He who is a householder, suitable to beg of, a donor, O Magha,'—so said Bhagavat,—'who, desirous of good, offers having what is good in view and giving to others in this world food and drink, such a one will prosper with those worthy of offerings.'

'He who is a householder, suitable to beg of, a donor' —so said the young man,—'who, desirous of good offers having what is good in view, and giving to others in this world food and drink,—tell me, I being such a one, O Bhagavat, of those worthy of offerings.'

Bhagavat: 'Those indeed who wander about in the world without clinging to anything and without possessing anything, perfect, self-restrained, on such in due time people should bestow oblations; let the Brahmin who has good works in view, offer.

'Those who have cut through all bonds and fetters, who are subdued, liberated, free from pain, and free from desire, on such in due time people should bestow oblations; let the Brahmin who has good works in view, offer.

'Those who are released from all bonds, who are subdued, liberated, free from pain, and free from desire, on such in due time people should bestow oblations; let the Brahmin who has good works in view, offer.

'Those who, having forsaken both passion and hatred and folly, have destroyed their desires, and lead a religious life, on such in due time people should bestow oblations; let the Brahmin who has good works in view, offer.

'Those in whom there lives no deceit, no arrogance, who are free from cupidity, free from selfishness, free from

The Temple of Bodh Gaya where Lord Buddha gained enlightenment

desire, on such in due time people should bestow oblations; let the Brahmin who has good works in view, offer.

'Those indeed who without being lost in craving, after crossing the stream of existence wander about free from selfishness, on such in due time people should bestow oblations; let the Brahmin who has good works in view, offer.

'Those in whom there is no craving for anything in the world, nor for existence after existence here or in the other world, on such in due time people should bestow oblations; let the Brahmin who has good works in view, offer.

'Those who, after leaving sensual pleasures, wander about houseless, well restrained, being like a straight shuttle, on such in due time people should bestow oblations; let the Brahmin who has good works in view, offer.

'Those whose passions are gone, whose senses are well composed, who are liberated like the moon out of the grasp of Rahu, on such in due time people should bestow oblations; let the Brahmin who has good works in view, offer.

'Those who are calm, whose passions are gone, who are without anger, and for whom there is no transmigration after having left here, on such in due time people should bestow oblations; let the Brahmina who has good works in view, offer.

'Those who, after leaving birth and death altogether, have conquered all doubt, on such in due time people should bestow oblations; let the Brahmin who has good works in view, offer.

'Those who wander about in the world with themselves for a light, not possessed of anything, in every respect liberated, on such in due time people should bestow oblations; let the Brahmin who has good works in view, offer.

'Those who in this world rightly understand this: "This is the last birth, there is no rebirth," on such in due time people should bestow oblations; let the Brahmin who has good works in view, offer.

'He who is accomplished, and delights in meditation, thoughtful, possessed of thorough enlightenment, a refuge for many, on such a one in due time people should bestow oblations; let the Brahmin who has good work in view, offer.'

'Certainly my question was not in vain, Bhagavat has told me of those worthy of offerings; for thou truly knowest this in this world, as surely to thee this Dhamma is known.

'He who is a householder, suitable to beg of, a donor,'—so said the young man Magha,—'who, desirous of good, offers having what is good in view, and giving to others in this world food and drink,—tell me I being such a one, O Bhagavat, of the blessing of offering.'

'Offer, O Magha,'—so said Bhagavat,—'and while offering make calm thy mind in all things; the object of the one that offers is the oblation, standing fast in this he leaves sin behind.

'Such a one whose passion is gone will repress hatred, cultivating an unbounded friendly mind; continually strenuous night and day he will spread infinite goodness through all regions.'

Magha: 'Who prospers? who is liberated and who is bound? In which way can one by himself go to Brahmaloka? Tell this to me who does not know, O Muni, when asked. Bhagavat is indeed my witness that Brahmin is seen by me today, for thou art to us equal to Brahmin, this is the truth; how can one attain Brahmaloka, O thou glorious one?'

'He who offers the threefold blessing of oblation, O Magha,'—so said Bhagavat,—'such a one will prosper with those worthy of offerings; so, having offered properly, he who is suitable to beg of, attains Brahmaloka, so I say.'

This having been said, Magha the young man spoke as follows to Bhagavat: 'Excellent, O venerable Gotama! Excellent, O venerable Gotama! As one raises what has been overthrown, or reveals what has been hidden, or tells the way to him who has gone astray, or holds out an oil lamp in the dark that those who have eyes may see the objects, even so by the venerable Gotama in manifold ways the Dhamma has been illustrated; I take refuge in the venerable Gotama and in the Dhamma and in the Sangh of Bhikkhus. Let the venerable Gotama accept me as a follower, who henceforth for all my life have taken refuge in him.'

6.

Six Famous Teachers of No Use

(Sabhiya Sutta)

Sabhiya, the Paribbajaka, goes to the six famous teachers of his time to have his questions answered, but not having his doubts solved, he repairs to Gotama and asks him how one is to behave to become a Brahmin, a Samana, a Nahataka, a Khettajina, a Kusala, a Pandita, a Muni, a Vedagu, an Anuvidita, a Dhira, an Ajaniya, a Sottiya, an Ariya, a Charanavat, a Paribbajaka. Bhagavat answers his questions, and Sabhiya finally receives the robe and the orders from Buddha.

So it was heard by me:

At one time Bhagavat dwelt at Rajagaha, in Veluvana, in Kalandakanivapa. And at that time questions were recited to Sabhiya, the Paribbajaka, wandering mendicant by a deity who had in a former birth been a relation of his: 'He who, O Sabhiya, be it a Samana or a Brahmin, explains these questions to thee when asked, near him thou shouldst live a religious life.'

Then Sabhiya, the Paribbajaka, having the questions from that deity, went to whatever Samanas and Brahmins there were that had an assembly of Bhikkhus, a crowd of followers and were well known teachers, famous leaders, considered excellent by the multitude, as Purana-Kassapa,

**The Tomb of Lumbini,
where Lord Buddha was born.**

Makkhali-Gosala, Ajita-Kesakambali, Pakudha Kachchayana, Sanjaya-Belatthiputta, and Nigantha-Nataputta. Those he went to, and after going to them, he asked the questions. They, being asked the questions by Sabhiya, the Paribbajaka, did not succeed in answering them, and not succeeding they showed wrath and hatred and discontent, and they also in return put questions to Sabhiya, the Paribbajaka,

Then this came to the mind of Sabhiya, the Paribbajaka: 'Whatever Samanas and Brahmins there are that have an assembly of Bhikkhus, a crowd of followers, and are well-known teachers, famous leaders, considered excellent by the multitude, as Purana-Kassapa, Makkhali-Gosala, Ajita-Kesakambali, Pakudha-Kachchayana, Sanjaya-Belatthiputta, and Nigantha-Nataputta, they, being asked questions by me, did not succeed in answering them and not succeeding they showed wrath and hatred and discontent, and they also in return put questions to me in this matter; surely I think I shall go back to what I have left, and enjoy sensual pleasures.'

Then this came to the mind of Sabhiya, the Paribbajaka: 'This Samana Gotama has both an assembly of Bhikkhus and a crowd of followers, and is a well-known teacher, a famous leader, considered excellent by the multitude, surely I think I shall go to Samana Gotama and ask these questions.' Then this came to the mind of Sabhiya, the Paribbajaka: 'Whatever Samanas and Brahmins there are that are decayed, old, aged, advanced in years, having reached old age, experienced elders, long ordained, having assemblies of Bhikkhus, crowds of followers, being teachers well known, famous leaders, considered excellent by the multitude, as Purana-Kassapa, Makkhali-Gosala, Ajita-Kesakambali, Pakudha-Kachchayana, Sanjaya-Belatthiputta, and Nigantha-Nataputta, they, being asked questions by me, did not succeed in answering them, and not succeeding they showed wrath and hatred and discontent, and they also in return put questions to me in this matter; I should like to know whether Samana Gotama being asked these questions will be able to explain them to me, for Samana Gotama is both young by birth and new in ascetic life.'

Then this came to the mind of Sabhiya, the Paribbajaka: 'Samana Gotama is not to be slighted because he is young; even if the Samana is young, yet he is mighty and powerful; surely I think I shall go to Samana Gotama and ask these questions.' Then Sabhiya, the Paribbajaka, went on a journey to Rajagaha, and wandering on his journey in regular order he came to Rajagaha, Veluvana Kalandakanivapa, to Bhagavat, and having come to Bhagavat he talked pleasantly with him and after having had some pleasant and remarkable conversation with him he sat down apart; sitting down apart Sabhiya, the Paribbajaka, spoke to Bhagavat in stanzas:

'Anxious and doubtful I have come,'—so said Sabhiya,—'longing to ask questions. Do thou put an end to these doubts when asked these questions by me, in regular order, and rightly explain them to me.'

'Thou hast come from afar, O Sabhiya,'—so said Bhagavat,—'longing to ask questions; I shall put an end to those doubts when asked those questions by thee, in regular order, and rightly I shall explain them to thee.

'Ask me, O Sabhiya, a question; whatsoever thou wishest in thy mind, that question I will explain, and put an end to thy doubt.'

Then this came to the mind of Sabhiya, the Paribbajaka: 'It is marvellous, it is wonderful indeed, the reception which I did not get from other Samanas and Brahmins has been given me by Gotama,' so saying he glad, rejoicing, delighted, and highly elated asked Bhagavat a question:

'What should a man necessarily have obtained that people may call him a Bhikkhu?' —so said Sabhiya,—'how may they call him compassionate, and how subdued? how can he be called enlightened Buddha? Asked about this do thou, Bhagavat, explain it to me.'

'He who by the path he has himself made, O Sabhiya,' —so said Bhagavat,—'has attained to perfect happiness, who has conquered doubt, who lives after having left behind both misfortune and fortune, who has destroyed rebirth, he is a Bhikkhu.

'Always resigned and attentive, he will not hurt anyone in all the world, the Samana who has crossed the stream of existence, and is untroubled, for whom there are no desires, he is compassionate.

'He whose senses are tamed internally and externally in all the world, he who after penetrating this and the other world longs for death, being trained, he is subdued.

'Whosoever, after having considered all times, the revolution, Samsara, both the vanishing and re-appearance of beings, is free from defilement, free from sin, is pure, and has obtained destruction of birth, him they call enlightened.

Then Sabhiya, the Paribbajaka, having approved of and rejoiced at the words of Bhagavat, glad, rejoicing, delighted, highly elated, asked Bhagavat another question:

'What should a man necessarily have obtained that people may call him a Brahmin?' —so said Sabhiya,—'and how may they call him a Samana? and how a Nahataka? how can he be called a Naga? Asked about this do thou, Bhagavat, explam it to me:

'He who, after removing all sins, O Sabhiya,' —so said Bhagavat,—'is immaculate, well composed, firm-minded, perfect after crossing the Samsara, such an independent one is called a Brahmin.

'He who is calm, having left behind good and evil, free from defilement, having understood this and the other world, and conquered birth and death, such a one is called a Samana by being so.

'Whosoever, after having washed away all sins internally and externally in all the world, does not enter time amongst gods and men who are subject to time, him they call a Nahataka, cleansed.

'He who does not commit any crime in the world, who, after abandoning all bonds and fetters, clings to nothing, being liberated, such a one is called a Naga, sinless, by being so.'

Then Sabhiya, the Paribbajaka, having approved of and rejoiced at the words of Bhagavat, glad, rejoicing, delighted, highly elated, further asked Bhagavat a question:

'Whom do the Buddhas call a Khettajina?'—so said Sabhiya,—'how can they call any one a Kusala, happy? and how a Pandita? how can he be called a Muni? Asked about this do thou, Bhagavat, explain it to me.'

'He who, after examining all regions, O Sabhiya,'—so said Bhagavat,—'the divine and the human, and Brahmin's region, is delivered from the radical bond of all regions, such a one is called a Khettajina, he who has conquered the regions by being so.

'He who, after examining all treasures, the divine and the human, and Brahmin's treasure, is delivered from the radical bond of all treasures, such a one is called a Kusala, by being so.

'He who, after examining both kinds of senses, internally and externally, is endowed with a clear understanding and has conquered evil and good, such a one is called a Pandita, wise, by being so.

'He who, having understood the Dhamma of the just and the unjust, internally and externally, in all the world, is to be worshipped by gods and men he, after breaking through the net of ties, is called a Muni, sage.'

Then Sabhiya, the Paribbajaka, having approved of and rejoiced at the words of Bhagavat, glad, rejoicing, delighted, highly elated, further asked Bhagavat a question:

'What should one necessarily have obtained that people may call him Vedagu?'—so said Sabhiya,—'and how may they call him Anuvidita? and how Viriyavat? How does one become Ajaniya? Asked about this do thou, O Bhagavat, explain it to me.'

'He who, having conquered all sensations, O Sabhiya,' —so said Bhagavat,—'which are known to Samanas and to Brahmins, is free from passion for all sensations, he is Vedagu, having passed sensation after conquering all sensation.

'He who, having seen the delusion of name and form, internally and externally, the root of sickness, and is delivered from the radical bond of all sickness, such a one is called Anuvidita, well-informed, by being so.

'He who is disgusted in this world with all sins, is strong after conquering the pain of hell, is strong and powerful, such a one is called Dhira or Viriyavat, firm, by being so.

'He whose bonds are cut off internally and externally, the root of ties, who is delivered from the radical bond of all ties, such a one is called Ajaniya, high-bred, by being so.'

Then Sabhiya, the Paribbajaka, having approved of and rejoiced at the words of Bhagavat, glad, rejoicing, delighted, highly elated, further asked Bhagavat a question:

'What should a man necessarily have obtained that people may call him a Sottiya?'—so said Sabhiya,—'how may they call him an Ariya? and how a Charanavat? how may he become a Paribbajaka? Asked about this do thou, O Bhagavat, explain it to me.'

'Whosoever, after having heard and understood every Dhamma in the world, O Sabhiya,'—so said Bhagavat, —whatsoever is wrong and whatsoever is blameless, is victorious, free from doubt, liberated, free from pain in every respect, him they call a Sottiya, learned in the revelation.

'Whosoever, after having cut off passions and desires, is wise and does not again enter the womb, having driven away the threefold sign, the mud of lust, and who does not again enter time (kappa), him they call an Ariya, noble.

'He who in this world, after having attained the highest gain in the Charanas, is skilful, has always understood the Dhamma, clings to nothing, is liberated, and for whom there are no passions, he is a Charanavat, endowed with the observances.

'Whosoever abstains from the action that has a painful result, above and below and across and in the middle, who wanders with understanding, who has put an end to deceit, arrogance, cupidity and anger, name and form, him they call a Paribbajaka, a wandering mendicant, who has attained the highest gain.'

Then Sabhiya, the Paribbajaka, having approved of and rejoiced at the words of Bhagavat, glad, rejoicing, delighted, highly elated, having risen from his seat, and having put his upper robe upon one shoulder, bending his joined hands towards Bhagavat, praised Bhagavat face to face in appropriate stanzas:

'Having conquered the three and sixty philosophical views referring to the disputations of the Samanas, thou hast crossed over the darkness of the stream.

'Thou hast passed to the end of and beyond pain, thou art a saint, perfectly enlightened, I consider thee one that has destroyed his passions, thou art glorious, thoughtful, of great understanding, O thou who puts an end to pain, thou hast carried me across.

'Because thou sawest my longing, and carriedst me across my doubt, adoration be to thee, O Muni, who hast attained the highest gain in the ways of wisdom; O thou who art a true kinsman of the Adichchas, thou art compassionate.

'The doubt I had before thou hast cleared away for me, O thou clearly-seeing; surely thou art a Muni, perfectly enlightened, there is no obstacle for thee.

'And all thy troubles are scattered and cut off, thou art calm, subdued, firm, truthful.

'All gods and both Narada and Pabbata rejoice at thee the chief of the sinless, Naganaga, the great hero, when thou art speaking.

'Adoration be to thee, O noble man, adoration be to thee, O thou best of men; in the world of men and gods there is no man equal to thee.

'Thou art Buddha, thou art the Master, thou art the Muni that conquers Mara; after having cut off desire thou hast crossed over and hast carried across this generation.

'The elements of existence are overcome by thee, the passions are destroyed by thee, thou art a lion, free from desire, thou hast left behind fear and terror.

'As a beautiful lotus does not adhere to the water, so thou dost not cling to good and evil, to either; stretch forth thy feet, O hero, Sabhiya worships the Master's feet.'

Then Sabhiya,the Paribbajaka, stooping with his head to Bhagavat's feet, said this to Bhagavat:

'It is excellent, O venerable! It is excellent, O venerable! As one raises what has been overthrown, or reveals what has been hidden, or tells the way to him who has gone astray, or holds out an oil lamp in the dark that those who have eyes may see the objects, even so by the venerable Gotama in manifold ways the Dhamma has been illustrated; I take refuge in the venerable Gotama, in the Dhamma, and in the Sangh of Bhikkhus; I wish to receive the robe and the orders from the venerable Bhagavat.'

'He who, O Sabhiya, formerly belonging to another creed, wishes to be adopted into this religion, Dhammavinaya, and wishes to receive the robe and the orders, he serves for four months; after the lapse of four months Bhikkhus who have appeased their thoughts will give him the robe and the orders to become a Bhikkhu, for I also in this matter acknowledge a difference of persons.'

'If, O venerable, those that formerly belonged to another creed and wish to be adopted into this religion and to receive the robe and the orders, serve for four months, and after the lapse of four months, Bhikkhus who have appeased their thoughts give them the robe and the orders that they may become Bhikkhus, I will serve for four years, and after the lapse of four years, Bhikkhus who have appeased their thoughts shall give me the robe and the orders that I may become a Bhikkhu.'

Sabhiya, the Paribbajaka, received the robe and the orders from Bhagavat, and the venerable Sabhiya, having lately received the Upasampada, leading a solitary, retired, strenuous, ardent, energetic life, lived after having in a short time in this existence by his own understanding ascertained and possessed himself of that highest perfection of a religious life for the sake of which men of good family rightly wander away from their houses to a houseless state. 'Birth had been destroyed, a religious life had been led, what was to be done had been done, there was nothing else to be done for this existence,' so he perceived, and the venerable Sabhiya became one of the saints.

7.

Sela Joins the Sangh

(Sela Sutta)

Keniya, the Jatila, invites Buddha with his assembly to take his meals with him on the morrow. Sela, the Brahmin, arrived at that place with his three hundred young men; seeing the preparations he asks what is going on, and is answered that Buddha is expected the next day. On hearing the word 'Buddha,' Sela asks where Buddha lives, goes to him, converses with him, and is converted; so are his followers.

So it was heard by me:

At one time, Bhagavat wandering about in Anguttarapa, with a large assembly of Bhikkhus, with 1250 Bhikkhus, went to Apana, a town in Anguttarapa.

And Keniya, the ascetic, with matted hair, Jatila, heard the following: 'The Samana, the venerable Gotama, the Sakya son, gone out from the family of the Sakyas, wandering about in Anguttarapa with a large assembly of Bhikkhus, with 1250 Bhikkhus, has reached Apana, and the following good praising words met the venerable Gotama: "And so he is Bhagavat, the venerable, the perfectly enlightened, endowed with knowledge and works, Vijjakarana, the happy, knowing the world, the incomparable, the charioteer of men that are to be subdued, the master, the enlightened of gods and men, the glorious; he teaches this world and the world of gods, of Maras, of Brahmins, and beings comprising Samanas and Brahmins, gods and men, having himself known and seen them face to face; he teaches the Dhamma which is good in the beginning, in the middle, and in the end, is full of meaning and rich in words, quite complete; he teaches a perfectly pure religious life, and good is the sight of such saints."

Then Keniya, the Jatila, went to the place where Bhagavat was, and having gone there he talked pleasantly with him, and after having had some pleasant and remarkable conversation with him he sat down apart; and while Keniya, the Jatila, was sitting down apart, Bhagavat, by rellgious talk, taught, advised, roused, and delighted him. Then Keniya, the Jatila, having been taught, advised, roused, and delighted by Bhagavat through religious talk, said this to Bhagavat:

'Let the venerable Gotama accept my food tomorrow, together with the assembly of Bhikkhus.'

This having been said, Bhagavat answered Keniya, the Jatila: 'Large, O Keniya, is the assembly of Bhikkhus, one thousand two hundred and fifty Bhikkhus, and thou art intimate with the Brahmins.'

A Monk Paying Homage to Lord Buddha, Cave 10

A second time Keniya, the Jatila, said this to Bhagavat: 'Although, O venerable Gotama, the assembly of Bhikkhus is large, one thousand two hundred and fifty Bhikkhus, and I am intimate with the Brahmins, let the venerable Gotama accept my food tomorrow, together with the assembly of Bhikkhus.'

A second time Bhagavat said this to Keniya, the Jatila: 'Large, O Keniya, is the assembly of Bhikkhus, one thousand two hundred and fifty Bhikkhus, and thou art intimate with the Brahmins.'

A third time Keniya, the Jatila, said this to Bhagavat: 'Although, O venerable Gotama, the assembly of Bhikkhus is large, one thousand two hundred and fifty Bhikkhus, and I am intimate with the Brahmins, yet let the venerable Gotama accept my food tomorrow together with the assembly of Bhikkhus.' Bhagavat assented by being silent.

Then Keniya, the Jatila, having learnt the assent of Bhagavat, after rising from his seat went to his hermitage, and having gone there he addressed his friends and servants, relatives and kinsmen as follows: 'Let my venerable friends and servants, relatives and kinsmen hear me:—the Samana Gotama has been invited by me to take his food with me tomorrow, together with the assembly of Bhikkhus: wherefore you must render me bodily service.'

'Surely, O venerable one,' so saying the friends and servants, relatives and kinsmen of Keniya, the Jatila, complying with his request, some of them dug fireplaces, some chopped firewood, some washed the vessels, some placed waterpots, some prepared seats. Keniya, the Jatila, on the other hand, himself provided a circular pavilion.

At that time the Brahmin Sela lived at Apana, perfect in the three Vedas, vocabulary, Ketubha, etymology, Itihasa as the fifth Veda, versed in metre, a grammarian, one not deficient in popular controversy and the signs of a great man, he taught three hundred young men the hymns. At that time Keniya, the Jatila, was intimate with the Brahmin Sela. Then the Brahmin Sela surrounded by three hundred young men, walking on foot, arrived at the place where the hermitage of Keniya, the Jatila, was. And the Brahmin Sela saw, the Jatilas in Keniya's hermitage, some of them digging fireplaces, some chopping firewood, some washing the vessels, some placing waterpots, some preparing seats, and Keniya, the Jatila, on the other hand, himself providing a circular pavilion; seeing Keniya, the Jatila, he said this: 'Is the venerable Keniya to celebrate the marriage of a son or the marriage of a daughter, or is there a great sacrifice at hand, or has Bimbisara, the king of Magadha, who has a large body of troops, been invited for tomorrow, together with his army?'

'I am not to celebrate the marriage of a son or the marriage of a daughter, nor has Bimbisara, the king of Magadha, who has a large body of troops, been invited for tomorrow, together with his army, yet a great sacrifice of mine is at hand. The Samana Gotama, the Sakya son, gone out from the Sakya family, wandering about in Anguttarapa with a large assembly of Bhikkhus, one thousand two hundred and fifty Bhikkhus, has reached Apana, and the following good praising words met the venerable Gotama: "And so he is Bhagavat, the venerable, the perfectly enlightened, endowed with knowledge and works Vijjakarana, the happy, knowing the world, the incomparable, the charioteer of men that are to be subdued, the master, the enlightened of gods and men, the glorious, he has been invited by me for tomorrow, together with the assembly of Bhikkhus."

'Didst thou say that he is a Buddha, O venerable Keniya?'

'Yes, I say, O venerable Sela, that he is a Buddha.'

'Didst thou say that he is a Buddha, O venerable Keniya?'

'Yes, I say, O venerable Sela, that he is a Buddha.'

Then this occurred to the Brahmin Sela: 'This sound

"Buddha" is indeed rare, but in our hymns are to be found the thirty-two signs of a great man, and for a great man endowed with these there are two conditions and no more: if he lives in a house he is a king, a universal king, a just religious king, a lord of the four-cornered earth, a conqueror, one who has obtained the security of his people and is possessed of the seven gems. These are his seven gems, namely, the wheel gem, the elephant gem, the horse gem, the pearl gem, the woman gem, the householder gem, and the chief gem as the seventh. He has more than a thousand sons, heroes, possessing great bodily strength and crushing foreign armies; he having conquered this ocean-girt earth without a rod and without a weapon, but by justice, lives in a house. But if, on the other hand, he goes out from his house to the houseless state, he becomes a saint, a perfectly enlightened, one who has removed the veil in the world. And where, O venerable Keniya, dwells now that venerable Gotama, the saint and the perfectly enlightened?'

This having been said, Keniya, the Jatila, stretching out his right arm, spoke as follows to the Brahmin Sela: 'There, where yon blue forest line is, O venerable Sela.'

Then the Brahmin Sela together with his three hundred young men went to the place where Bhagavat was. Then the Brahmin Sela addressed those young men: 'Come ye, venerable ones, with but little noise, walking step by step, for Bhagavats are difficult of access, walking alone like lions, and when I speak to the venerable Samana Gotama, do ye not utter interrupting words, but wait ye venerable ones, for the end of my speech.'

Then the Brahmin Sela went to the place where Bhagavat was, and having gone there he talked pleasantly with Bhagavat, and after having had some pleasant and remarkable conversation with him he sat down apart, and while sitting down apart Sela, the Brahmin, looked for the thirty-two signs of a great man on the body of Bhagavat.

And the Brahmin Sela saw the thirty-two signs of a great man on the body of Bhagavat with the exception of two; in respect to two of the signs of a great man he had doubts, he hesitated, he was not satisfied, he was not assured as to the member being enclosed in a membrane and as to his having a large tongue.

Then this occurred to Bhagavat: 'This Brahmin Sela sees in me the thirty-two signs of a great man with the exception of two, in respect to two of the signs of a great man he has doubts, he hesitates, he is not satisfied, he is not assured as to the member being enclosed in a membrane, and as to my having a large tongue.' Then Bhagavat created such a miraculous creature that the Brahmin Sela might see Bhagavat's member enclosed in a membrane. Then Bhagavat having put out his tongue touched and stroked both his ears, touched and stroked both nostrils, and the whole circumference of his forehead he covered with his tongue.

Then this occurred to the Brahmin Sela: 'The Samana Gotama is endowed with the thirty-two signs of a great man, with them all, not with only some of them, and yet I do not know whether he is a Buddha or not; I have heard from old and aged Brahmins, teachers and their previous teachers, that those who are saints and perfectly enlightened, manifest themselves when their praise is uttered. I think I shall praise the Samana Gotama face to face in suitable stanzas.' Then thc Brahmin Sela praised Bhagavat face to face in suitable stanzas:

'Thou hast a perfect body, thou art resplendent, well-born, of beautiful aspect, thou hast a golden colour, O Bhagavat, thou hast very white teeth, thou art strong.

'All the signs that are for a well-born man, they are on thy body, the signs of a great man.

'Thou hast a bright eye, a handsome countenance, thou art great, straight, majestic, thou shinest like a sun in the midst of the assembly of the Samanas.

'Thou art a Bhikkhu of a lovely appearance, thou hast a skin like gold; what is the use of being a Samana to thee who art possessed of the highest beauty?

'Thou deservest to be a king, a king of universal kings, a ruler of the four-cornered earth, a conqueror, a lord of the Jambu grove.

'Khattiyas and wealthy kings are devoted to thee; rule, O Gotama, as a king of kings, a leader of men.'

'I am a king, O Sela,'—so said Bhagavat,—'an incomparable, religious king , with justice I turn the wheel, a wheel that is irresistible.'

'Thou acknowledgest thyself to be perfectly enlightened,'—so said Sela, the Brahmin,—'an incomparable, religious king; "with Justice I turn the wheel," so thou sayest, O Gotama.

'Who is thy general, who is thy disciple, who is the successor of the master, who is to turn after thee the wheel of religion turned by thee?'

'The wheel is turned by me, O Sela,'—so said Bhagavat, —'the incomparable wheel of Law, Sariputta is to turn after me, he taking after Tathagata.

'What is to be known is known by me, what is to be cultivated is cultivated by me, what is to be left is left by me, therefore I am a Buddha, O Brahmin.

'Subdue thy doubt about me, have faith in me, O Brahmin, difficult to obtain is the sight of Buddhas repeatedly.

'Of those whose manifestation is difficult for you to obtain in the world repeatedly, I am, O Brahmin, a perfectly enlightened, an incomparable physician,

'Most eminent, matchless, a crusher of Mara's army; having subjected all enemies I rejoice secure on every side.'

Sela to his followers : '0 venerable ones, pay attention to this: as the clearly-seeing Buddha says, so it is: he is a physician, a great hero, and roars like a lion in the forest.

'Who, having seen him, the most eminent, the matchless, the crusher of Mara's army, is not appeased, even if he be of black origin.

'He who likes me, let him follow after me, he who does not like me, let him go away; I shall at once take the orders in presence of him of excellent understanding, Buddha.'

The followers of Sela: 'If this doctrine of the enlightened pleases thee, we also shall take the orders in the presence of him of excellent understanding.'

Sela: 'These three hundred Brahmins ask with clasped hands to be admitted into the order: we want to cultivate a religious life, O Bhagavat, in thy presence.'

'A religious life is well taught by me,—O Sela,' so said Bhagavat,—'an instantaneous, an immediate life in which it is not in vain to become an ascetic to one who learns in earnest.'

Then the Brahmin Sela together with his assembly took the robe and the orders in the presence of Bhagavat.

Then Keniya, the Jatila, by the expiration of that night, having provided in his hermitage nice hard food and soft food, let Bhagavat know the time of the meal: 'It is time, O venerable Gotama, the meal is prepared.' Then Bhagavat in the morning, having put on his raiment and taken his bowl and robes, went to the Jatila Keniya's hermitage, and having gone there he sat down on the prepared seat, together with the assembly of Bhikkhus. Then Keniya, the Jatila, satisfied and served with his own hands the assembly of Bhikkhus, with Buddha at their head, with nice hard food and soft food. Then Keniya, the Jatila, having gone up to Bhagavat who had finished eating and had taken his hand out of the bowl, took a low seat and sat down apart, and while Keniya, the Jatila, was sitting down apart, Bhagavat delighted him with these stanzas:

'The principal thing in sacrifice is the sacred fire, the principle thing amongst the hymns is the Savitti, the king is the principal amongst men, and the sea the principal amongst waters.

'Amongst the stars the moon is the principal thing, the sun is the principal thing amongst the burning objects, amongst those that wish for good works and make offerings the Sangh indeed is the principal.'

Then Bhagavat, having delighted Keniya, the Jatila, with these stanzas, rose from his seat and went away.

Then the venerable Sela together with his assembly leading a solitary, retired, strenuous, ardent, energetic life, lived after having in a short time in this existence by his own understanding ascertained and possessed himself of that highest perfection of a religious life for the sake of which men of good family rightly wander away from their houses to a houseless state; birth had been destroyed, a religious life had been led, what was to be done had been done, there was nothing else to be done for this existence, so he perceived, and the venerable Sela together with his assembly became one of the saints.

Then the venerable Sela together with his assembly went to Bhagavat, and having gone to him he put his upper robe on one shoulder, and bending his joined hands towards Bhagavat, he addressed him in stanzas:

'Because we took refuge in thee on the eighth day previous to this, O thou clearly-seeing, in seven nights, O Bhagavat, we have been trained in thy doctrine.

'Thou art Buddha, thou art the Master, thou art the Muni that conquered Mara, thou hast, after a cutting off the affections, crossed over the stream of existence and taken over these beings.

'The elements of existence have been overcome by thee, the passions have been destroyed by thee, thou art a lion not seizing on anything, thou hast left behind fear and danger.

'These three hundred Bhikkhus stand here with clasped hands; stretch out thy feet, O hero, let the Nagas worship the Master's feet.'

8.

The Terms of the World

(Salla Sutta)

Life is short, mortals are subject to death, but knowing the terms of the world the wise do not grieve, and those who have left sorrow will be blessed.

Without a cause and unknown is the life of mortals in this world, troubled and brief, and combined with pain.

For there is not any means by which those that have been born can avoid dying; after reaching old age there is death, of such a nature are living beings.

As ripe fruits are early in danger of falling, so mortals when born are always in danger of death.

As all earthen vessels made by the potter end in being broken, so is the life of mortals.

Both young and grown-up men, both those who are fools and those who are wise men, all fall into the power of death, all are subject to death.

Of those who, overcome by death, go to the other world, a father does not save his son, nor relatives their relations.

Mark! while relatives are looking on and lamenting greatly, one by one of the mortals is carried off like an ox that is going to be killed.

So the world is afflicted with death and decay, therefore the wise do not grieve, knowing the terms of the world.

For him, whose way thou dost not know, either when he is coming or when he is going, not seeing both ends, thou grievest in vain.

If he who grieves gains anything, although he is only a fool hurting himself, let the wise man do the same.

Not from weeping nor from grieving will any one obtain peace of mind; on the contrary, the greater his pain will be, and his body will suffer.

He will be lean and pale, hurting himself by himself, and yet the dead are not kept alive, lamentation therefore is of no avail.

He who does not leave grief behind, goes only deeper into pain; bewailing the dead he falls into the power of grief.

Look at others passing away, men that go to what they deserve according to their deeds, beings trembling already here, after falling into the power of death.

In whatever manner people think it will come to pass, different from that it beçomes, so great is the disappointment in this world; see, such are the terms of the world.

Even if a man lives a hundred years or even more, he is at last separated from the company of his relatives and leaves life in this world.

Therefore, let one, hearing the words of the saint subdue his lamentation; seeing the one that has passed away and is dead, let him say: 'He will not be found by me any more.'

As a house on fire is extinguished by water, so also the wise, sensible, learned, clever man rapidly drives away sorrow that has arisen, as the wind a tuft of cotton.

He who seeks his own happiness should draw out his arrow which is his lamentation, and complaint, and grief.

He who has drawn out the arrow and is not dependent on anything, he, having obtained peace of mind, and having overcome all sorrow, will become free from sorrow, and blessed.

Decoration on a Pillar, Cave 10

9.

Brahmin Not by Birth

(Vasettha Sutta)

A dispute arose between two young men, Bharadvaja and Vasettha, the former contending man to be a Brahmin by birth, the latter by deeds. They agreed to go and ask Samana Gotama, and he answered that man is a Brahmin by his work only. The two young men are converted.

So it was heard by me:

At one time Bhagavat dwelt at Ichchhanamkala, in the Ichchhanamkala forest. At that time many distinguished, wealthy Brahmins lived at Ichchhanamkala, as the Brahmin Chamkin, the Brahmin Tarukkha, the Brahmin Pokkharasati, the Brahmin Janussoni, the Brahmin Todeyya, and other distinguished, wealthy Brahmins.

Then this dialogue arose between the young men Vasettha and Bharadvaja while walking about:

'How does one become a Brahmin?'

The young man Bharadvaja said: 'When one is noble by birth on both sides, on the mother's and on the father's side, of pure conception up to the seventh generation of ancestors, not discarded and not reproached in point of birth, in this way one is a Brahmin.'

The young man Vasettha said: 'When one is virtuous and endowed with holy works, in this way he is a Brahmin.'

Neither could the young man Bharadvaja convince the young man Vasettha, nor could the young man Vasettha convince the young man Bharadvaja. Then the young man Vasettha addressed the young man Bharadvaja: 'O Bharadvaja, this Samana Gotama, the Sakya son, gone out from the Sakya family, dwells at Ichchhanamkala, in the forest of Ichchhanamkala, and the following good praising words met the venerable Gotama: 'And so he is Bhagavat, the venerable, the enlightened, the glorious, let us go, O venerable Bharadvaja, let us go to the place where the Samana Gotama is, and having gone there, let us ask the Samana Gotama about this matter, and as the Samana Gotama replies so will we understand it.'

'Very well, O venerable one;' so the young man Bharadvaja answered the young man Vasettha.

Then the young men Vasettha and Bharadvaja went to the place where Bhagavat was, and having gone, they talked pleasantly with Bhagavat, and after having had some pleasant and remarkable conversation with him they sat down apart. Sitting down apart the young man Vasettha addressed Bhagavat in stanzas:

'We are accepted and acknowledged masters of the three Vedas, I am a pupil of Pokkharasati, and this young man is the pupil of Tarukkha.

'We are accomplished in all the knowledge propounded by those who are acquainted with the three Vedas, we are versed in the metre, grammar, and equal to our teachers in recitation.

'We have a controversy regarding the distinctions of birth, O Gotama! Bharadvaja says, one is a Brahmin by birth, and I say, by deeds; know this, O thou clearly-seeing!

'We are both unable to convince each other, therefore, we have come to ask thee who are celebrated as perfectly enlightened.

'As people adoring the full moon worship her with uplifted clasped hands, so they worship Gotama in the world.

'We ask Gotama who has come as an eye to the world: Is a man a Brahmin by birth, or is he so by deeds? Tell us who do not know that we may know a Brahmin.'

'I will explain to you, O Vasettha,'—so said Bhagavat,—'in due order the exact distinction of living beings according to species, for their species are manifold.

'Know ye the grass and the trees, although they do not exhibit it, the marks that constitute species are for them, and their species are manifold.

'Then know ye the worms, and the moths, and the different sorts of ants, the marks that constitute species are for them, and their species are manifold.

'Know ye also the four-footed animals small and great, the marks that constitute species are for them, and their species are manifold.

'Know ye also the serpents, the long-backed snakes, the marks that constitute species are for them, and their species are manifold.

'Then know ye also the fish which range in the water, the marks that constitute species are for them, and their species are manifold.

'Then know ye also the birds that are borne along on wings and move through the air, the marks that constitute species are for them, and their species are manifold.

'As in these species the marks that constitute species are abundant, so in men the marks that constitute species are not abundant.

'Not as regards their hair, head, ears, eyes, mouth, nose, lips, or brows,

'Nor as regards their neck, shoulders, belly, back, hip, breast, female organ, sexual intercourse,

'Nor as regards their hands, feet, palms, nails, calves, thighs, colour, or voice are there marks that constitute species as in other species.

'Difference there is in beings endowed with bodies, but amongst men this is not the case, the difference amongst men is nominal only.

For whoever amongst men lives by cow-keeping,—know this, O Vasettha,—he is a husbandman, not a Brahmin.

'And whoever amongst men lives by different mechanical arts,—know this, O Vasettha, he is an artisan, not a Brahmin,

'And whoever amongst men lives by trade,—know this, O Vasettha,—he is a merchant, not a Brahmin.

Apsara, Sigiria, Srilanka

'And whoever amongst men lives by serving others, —know this, O Vasettha,—he is a servant, not a Brahmin.

'And whoever amongst men lives by theft,—know this, O Vasettha,—he is a thief, not a Brahmin.

'And whoever amongst men lives by archery,—know this, O Vasettha,—he is a soldier, not a Brahmin.

'And whoever amongst men lives by performing household ceremonials,—know this, O Vasettha,—he is a sacrificer, not a Brahmin.

'And whoever amongst men possesses villages and countries,—know this, O Vasettha,—he is a king, not a Brahmin.

'And I do not call one a Brahmin on account of his birth or of his origin from a particular mother; he may be called Bhovadi, and he may be wealthy, but the one who is possessed of nothing and seizes upon nothing, him I call a Brahmin.

'Whosoever, after cutting all bonds, does not tremble, has shaken off all ties and is liberated, him I call a Brahmin.

'The man who, after cutting the strap, i.e., enmity, the thong, i.e., attachment, and the rope, i.e., scepticism with all that pertains to it, has destroyed all obstacles' i.e., ignorance, the enlightened, Buddha, him I call a Brahmin.

'Whosoever, being innocent, endures reproach, blows, and bonds, the man who is strong in his endurance and has for his army this strength, him I call a Brahmin.

'The man who is free from anger, endowed with holy works, virtuous, without desire, subdued, and wearing the last body, him I call a Brahmin.

'The man who, like water on a lotus leaf, or a mustard seed on the point of a needle, does not cling to sensual pleasures, him I call a Brahmin.

'The man who knows in this world the destruction of his pain, who has laid aside his burden, and is liberated, him I call a Brahmin.

'The man who has a profound understanding, who is wise, who knows the true way and the wrong way, who has attained the highest good, him I call a Brahmin.

'The man who does not mix with householders nor with the houseless, who wanders about without a house and who has few wants, him I call a Brahmin.

'Whosoever, after refraining from hurting living creatures, both those that tremble and those that are strong, does not kill or cause to be killed, him I call a Brahmin.

'The man who is not hostile amongst the hostile, who is peaceful amongst the violent, not seizing upon anything amongst those that seize upon everything, him I call a Brahmin.

'The man whose passion and hatred, arrogance and hypocrisy have dropt like a mustard seed from the point of a needle, him I call a Brahmin.

'The man that utters true speech, instructive and free from harshness, by which he does not offend anyone, him I call a Brahmin.

'Whosoever in the world does not take what has not been given to him, be it long or short, small or large, good or bad, him I call a Brahmin.

'The man who has no desire for this world or the next, who is desireless and liberated, him I call a Brahmin.

The man who has no desire, who through his knowledge is free from doubt, and has attained the depth of immortality, him I call a Brahmin.

'Whosoever in this world has overcome good and evil, both ties, who is free from grief and defilement, and is pure, him I call a Brahmin.

'The man that is stainless like the moon, pure, serene, and undisturbed, who has destroyed joy, him I call a Brahmin.

'Whosoever has passed over this quagmire difficult to pass, who has passed over revolution (Samsara) and folly, who has crossed over, who has reached the other shore, who is meditative, free from desire and doubt, calm without seizing upon anything, him I call Brahmin.

'Whosoever in this world, after abandoning sensual pleasures, wanders about houseless, and has destroyed the existence of sensual pleasures, him I call a Brahmin.

'Whosoever in this world, after abandoning craving, wanders about houseless, and has destroyed the existence of desire, him I call a Brahmin.

'Whosoever, after leaving human attachment, has overcome divine attachment, and is liberated from all attachment, him I call a Brahmin.

'The man that, after leaving pleasure and disgust, is calm and free from the elements of existence, who is a hero, and has conquered all the world, him I call a Brahmin.

'Whosoever knows wholly the vanishing and reappearance of beings, does not cling to anything, is happy, and enlightened, him I call a Brahmin.

The man whose way neither gods nor Gandhabbas nor men know, and whose passions are destroyed, who is a saint, him I call a Brahmin.

'The man for whom there is nothing, neither before nor after nor in the middle, who possesses nothing, and does not seize upon anything, him I call a Brahmin.

'The man that is undaunted like a bull, who is eminent, a hero, a great sage, victorious, free from desire, purified, enlightened, him I call a Brahmin.

'The man who knows his former dwellings, who sees both heaven and hell, and has reached the destruction of births, him I call a Brahmin.

'For what has been designated as "name" and "family" in the world is only a term, what has been designated here and there is understood by common consent.

'Adhered to for a long time are the views of the ignorant, the ignorant tell us, one is Brahmin by birth.

'Not by birth is one a Brahmin, nor is one by birth no Brahmin; by work one is a Brahmin, by work one is no Brahmin.

'By work one is a husbandman, by work one is an artisan, by work one is a merchant, by work one is a servant.

'By work one is a thief, by work one is a soldier, by work one is a sacrificer, by work one is a king.

'So the wise, who see the cause of things and understand the result of work, know this work as it really is.

'By work the world exists, by work mankind exists, beings are bound by work as the linchpin of the rolling cart keeps the wheel on.

'By penance, by a religious life, by self-restraint, and by temperance, by this one is a Brahmin, such a one they call the best Brahmin.

'He who is endowed with the threefold knowledge, is calm and has destroyed regreneration,—know this, O Vasettha,—he is to the wise Brahmin and Sakka.'

This having been said, the young men Vasettha and Bharadvaja spoke to Bhagavat as follows:

'Is is excellent, O venerable Gotama! It is execllent. O venerable Gotama! As one raises what has been overthrown, or reveals what has been hidden, or tells the way to him who has gone astray, or holds out an oil lamp in the dark that those who have eyes may see the objects, even so by the venerable Gotama in manifold ways the Dhamma has been illustrated; we take refuge in the venerable Gotama, in the Dhamma, and in the Sangh of Bhikkhus; may the venerable Gotama receive us as followers, who from this day for life have taken refuge in him.'

10.

Guard Your Speech and Mind

(Kokaliya Sutta)

Kokaliya abuses Sariputta and Moggallana to Buddha; therefore as soon as he has left Buddha, he is struck with boils, dies and goes to the Paduma hell, whereupon Buddha describes to the Bhikkhus the punishment of backbiters in hell.

So it was heard by me:

At one time Bhagavat dwelt at Savatthi, in Jetavana, in the park of Anathapindika. Then the Bhikkhu Kokaliya approached Bhagavat, and after having approached and saluted Bhagavat he sat down apart; sitting down apart the Bhikkhu Kokaliya said this to Bhagavat: 'O thou venerable one, Sariputta and Moggallana have evil desires, they have fallen into the power of evil desires.'

When this had been said, Bhagavat spoke to the Bhikkhu Kokaliya as follows: 'Do not say so. Kokaliya; do not say so, Kokaliya; appease, O Kokaliya, thy mind in regard to Sariputta and Moggallana: Sariputta and Moggallana are amiable.'

A second time the Bhikkhu Kokaliya said this to Bhagavat: 'Although thou, O venerable Bhagavat, appear to me to be faithful and trustworthy, yet Sariputta and Moggallana have evil desires, they have fallen into the power of evil desires.'

A second time Bhagavat said this to the Bhikkhu Kokaliya: 'Do not say so, Kokaliya; do not say so, Kokaliya; appease, O Kokaliya, thy mind in regard to Sariputta and Moggallana: Sariputta and Moggallana are amiable.'

A third time the Bhikkhu Kokaliya said this to Bhagavat: 'Although thou, O venerable Bhagavat appear to me to be faithful and trustworthy yet Sariputta and Moggallana have evil desires, Sariputta and Moggallana have fallen into the power of evil desires.'

A third time Bhagavat said this to the Bhikkhu Kokaliya: 'Do not say so, Kokaliya; do not say so, Kokaliya; appease, O Kokaliya, thy mind in regard to Sariputta and Moggallana: Sariputta and Moggallana are amiable.'

Then the Bhikkhu Kokaliya, after having risen from his seat and saluted Bhagavat and walked round him towards the right, went away; and when he had been gone a short time, all his body was struck with boils as large as mustard seeds; after being only as large as mustard seeds, they became as large as kidney beans; after being only as large as kidney beans, they became as large as chick peas; after being only as large as chick peas, they became as large as a Kolatthi egg; after being only as large as a Kolatthi egg, they became as large as the jujube fruit; after being only as large as the jujube fruit, they became as large as the fruit of the emblic myrobalan; after being only as large as the emblic myrobalan, they became as large as the unripe beluva fruit; after being only as large as the unripe beluva fruit, they became as large as a billi fruit; after being as large as a billi fruit they broke, and matter and blood flowed out.

Then the Bhikkhu Kokaliya died of that disease, and when he had died the Bhikkhu Kokaliya went to the Paduma hell, having shown a hostile mind against Sariputta and Moggallana. Then when the night had passed, Brahmin Sahampati of a beautiful appearance, having lit up all Jetavana, approached Bhagavat, and having approached and saluted Bhagavat, he stood apart, and standing apart Brahmin Sahampati said this to Bhagavat: 'O thou venerable one, Kokaliya, the Bhikkhu, is dead; and after death, O thou venerable one, the Bhikkhu Kokaliya is gone to the Paduma hell, having shown a hostile mind against Sariputta and Moggallana.'

This said Brahmin Sahampati, and after saying this and saluting Bhagavat, and walking round him towards the right, he disappeared there.

Then Bhagavat, after the expiration of that night, addressed the Bhikkhus thus: 'Last night, O Bhikkhus, when the night had nearly passed, Brahmin Sahampati of a beautiful appearance, having lit up all Jetavana, approached Bhagavat, and having approached and saluted Bhagavat, he stood apart, and standing apart Brahmin Sahampati said this to Bhagavat: "O thou venerable one, Kokaliya, the Bhikkhu, is dead; and after death, O thou venerable one, the Bhikkhu Kokaliya is gone to the Paduma hell, having shown a hostile mind against Sariputta and Moggallana." This said Brahmin Sahampati, O Bhikkhus, and having said this and saluted me, and walked round me towards the right, he disappeared there.'

When this had been said, a Bhikkhu asked Bhagavat: 'How long is the rate of life, O venerable one, in the Paduma hell?'

'Long, O Bhikkhu, is the rate of life in the Paduma hell, it is not easy to calculate either by saying so many years or so many hundreds of years or so many thousands of years or so many hundred thousands of years.'

'But it is possible, I suppose, to make a comparison, O thou venerable one?'

'It is possible, O Bhikkhu;' so saying, Bhagavat spoke as follows: 'Even as, O Bhikkhu, if there were a Kosala load of sesamum seed containing twenty kharis, and a man after the lapse of every hundred years were to take from it one sesamum seed at a time, then that Kosala load of sesamum seed, containing twenty kharis would, O Bhikkhu, sooner by this means dwindle away and be used up than one Abbuda hell; and even as are twenty Abbuda hells, O Bhikkhu, so is one Nirabbuda hell; and even as are twenty Nirabbuda hells, O Bhikkhu, so is one Ababa hell; and even as are twenty Ababa hells, O Bhikkhu, so is one Ahaha hell; and even as are twenty Ahaha hells, O Bhikkhu, so is one Atata hell; and even as are twenty Atata hells, O Bhikkhu, so is one Kumuda hell;

The Empty Niche, the 5m. standing Buddha destroyed in the 21st Century, Kandhar.

and even as are twenty Kumuda hells, O Bhikkhu, so is one Sogandhika hell; and even as are twenty Sogandhika hells, O Bhikkhu, so is one Uppalaka hell; and even as are twenty Uppalaka hells, O Bhikkhu, so is one Pundarika hell; and even as are twenty Pundarika hells, O Bhikkhu, so is one Paduma hell; and to the Paduma hell, O Bhikkhu, the Bhikkhu Kokaliya is gone, having shown a hostile mind against Sariputta and Moggallana.' This said Bhagavat, and having said this Sugata, the Master, furthermore spoke as follows:

'To every man that is born, an axe is born in his mouth, by which the fool cuts himself, when speaking bad language.

'He who praises him who is to be blamed, or blames him who is to be praised, gathers up sin in his mouth, and through that sin he will not find any joy.

'Trifling is the sin that consists in losing riches by dice; this is a greater sin that corrupts the mind against Sugatas.

'Out of the one hundred thousand Nirabbudas he goes to thirty-six, and to five Abbudas; because he blames an Ariya he goes to hell, having employed his speech and mind badly.

'He who speaks falsely goes to hell, or he who having done something says, "I have not done it;" both these after death become equal, in another world they are both men guilty of a mean deed.

'He who offends an offenceless man, a pure man, free from sin, such a fool the evil deed reverts against, like fine dust thrown against the wind.

'He who is given to the quality of covetousness such a one censures others in his speech being himself unbelieving, stingy, wanting in affability, given to backbiting.

O thou foul-mouthed, false, ignoble, blasting, wicked, evildoing, low, sinful, base-born man, do not be garrulous in this world, else thou wilt be an inhabitant of hell.

'Thou spreadest pollution to the misfortune of others, thou revilest the just, committing sin yourself and having done many evil deeds thou wilt go to the pool of hell for a long time.

'For one's deeds are not lost, they will surely come back to you, their master will meet with them, the fool who commits sin will feel the pain in himself in the other world.

'To the place where one is struck with iron rods, to the iron stake with sharp edges he goes; then there is for him food as appropriate, resembling a red-hot ball of iron.

'For those who have anything to say there do not say fine things, they do not approach with pleasing faces; they do not find refuge from their sufferings, they lie on spread embers, they enter a blazing pyre.

'Covering them with a net they kill them there with iron hammers; they go to dense darkness, for that is spread out like the body of the earth.

'Then they enter an iron pot, they enter a blazing pyre, for they are boiled in those iron pots for a long time, jumping up and down in the pyre.

'Then he who commits sin is surely boiled in a mixture of matter and blood; whatever quarter he inhabits, he becomes rotten there from coming in contact with matter and blood.

'He who commits sin will surely be boiled in the water, the dwelling-place of worms; there it is not possible to get to the shore, for the jars are even all round.

'Again they enter the sharp Asipattavana with mangled limbs; having seized the tongue with a hook, the different watchmen of hell kill them.

'Then they enter Vetarani, that is difficult to cross and has got streams of razors with sharp edges; there the fools fall in, the evildcers after having done evil.

'There black, mottled flocks of ravens eat them who are weeping, and dogs, jackals, great vultures, falcons, crows tear them.

'Miserable indeed is the life here in hell which the man sees that commits sin. Therefore should a man in this world for the rest of his life be strenuous, and not indolent.

'Those loads of sesamum seed which are carried in Paduma hell have been counted by the wise, they are five nahutas of kotis and twelve hundred kotis (512,000,000,000) besides.

'As long as hells are called painful in this world, so long people will have to live there for a long time; therefore amongst those who have pure, amiable, and good qualities one should always guard speech and mind.'

11.

Such A Muni Deserves Wisdom

(Nalaka Sutta)

The Isi Asita, also called Kanhasiri, on seeing the gods rejoicing, asks the cause of it, and having heard that Buddha has been born, he descends from Tusita heaven. When the Sakyas showed the child to him, he received it joyfully and prophesied about it. Buddha explains to Nalaka, the sister's son of Asita, the highest state of wisdom.

The Isi Asita. saw in their resting-places during the day the joyful, delighted flocks of the Tidasa gods, and the gods in bright clothes, always highly praising Inda, after taking their clothes and waving them.

Seeing the gods with pleased minds, delighted, and showing his respect, he said this on that occasion: 'Why is the assembly of the gods so exceedingly pleased, why do they take their clothes and wave them?

'When there was an encounter with the Asuras, a victory for the gods and the Asuras were defeated, then there was not such a rejoicing. What wonderful thing have the gods seen that they are so delighted?

'They shout and sing and make music, they throw about their arms and dance. I ask you the inhabitants of the tops of mount Meru, remove my doubt quickly, O venerable ones!'

'The Bodhisatta, the execllent pearl, the incomparable, is born for the good and for a blessing in the world of men, in the town of the Sakyas, in the country of Lumbini. Therefore, we are glad and exceedingly pleased.

'He, the most excellent of all beings, the pre-eminent man, the bull of men, the most excellent of all creatures wIll turn the wheel of the Dhamma in the forest called after the Isis, he who is like the roaring lion, the strong lord of beasts.'

Having heard that noise he descended from the heaven of Tusita. Then he went to Suddhodana's palace, and having sat down there he said this to the Sakyas: 'Where is the prince? I wish to see him.'

Then the Sakyas showed to the Isi, called Asita, the child, the prince who was like shining gold, manufactured by a very skilful smith in the mouth of a forge, and beaming in glory and having a beautiful appearance.

Seeing the prince shining like fire, bright like the bull of stars wandering in the sky, like the burning sun in autumn, free from clouds, he joyfully obtained great delight.

The gods held in the sky a parasol with a thousand circles and numerous branches, yaks' tails with golden sticks were fanned, but those who held the yaks' tails and the parasol were not seen.

The Isi with the matted hair, by name Kanhasiri, on seeing the yellow blankets shining like a golden coin, and the white parasol held over his head, received him delighted and happy.

And having received the bull of the Sakyas, he who was wishing to receive him and knew the signs and the hymns, with pleased thoughts raised his voice, saying: 'Without superior is this, the most excellent of men.'

Then remembering his own migration he was displeased and shed tears; seeing this the Sakyas asked the weeping Isi, whether there would be any obstacle in the prince's path.

Seeing the Sakyas displeased the Isi said: 'I do not remember anything that will be unlucky for the prince, there will be no obstacles at all for him, for this is no inferior person. Be without anxiety.

'This prince will reach the summit of perfect enlightenment, he will turn the wheel of the Dhamma, he who sees what is exceedingly pure, i.e., Nibbana, this prince feels for the welfare of the multitude, and his religion will be widely spread.

'My life here will shortly be at an end, in the middle of his life there will be death for me; I shall not hear the Dhamma of the incomparable one; therefore I am afflicted, unfortunate, and suffering.'

Having afforded the Sakyas great joy he went out from the interior of the palace to lead a religious life; but taking pity on his sister's son, he induced him to embrace the Dhamma of the incomparable one.

'When thou hearest from others the sound "Buddha," or "he who has acquired perfect enlightenment, walks the way of the Dhamma," then going there and enquiring about the particulars, lead a religious life with that Bhagavat.'

Instructed by him, the friendly-minded, by one who saw in the future what is exceedingly pure, i.e., Nibbana, he, Nalaka, with a heap of gathered-up good works, and with guarded senses dwelt with him looking forward to Jina, i.e., Buddha.

Hearing the noise, while the excellent Jina turned the wheel of the Dhamma, and going and seeing the bull of the Isis, he, after being converted asked the eminent Muni about the best wisdom, when the time of Asita's order had come.

'These words of Asita are acknowledged true by me, therefore we ask thee, O Gotama, who art perfect in all things.

'O Muni, to me who am houseless, and who wish to embrace a Bhikkhu's life, explain when asked the highest state, the state of wisdom.'

'I will declare to thee the state of wisdom,'—so said Bhagavat,—'difficult to carry out, and difficult to obtain; come, I will explain it to thee, stand fast, be firm.

'Let a man cultivate equanimity: which is both reviled and praised in the village, let him take care not to corrupt his mind, let him live calm, and without pride.

'Various objects disappear, like a flame of fire in the wood; women tempt the Muni, let them not tempt him.

'Let him be disgusted with sexual intercourse having left behind sensual pleasures of all kinds being inoffensive and dispassionate towards living creatures, towards anything that is feeble or strong.

'As I am so are these, as these are so am I, identifying himself with others, let him not kill nor cause any one to kill.

'Having abandoned desire and covetousness let him act as one that sees clearly where a common man sticks, let him cross over this hell.

'Let him be with an empty stomach, taking little food, let him have few wants and not be covetous; not being consumed by desire he will without desire be happy.

'Let the Muni, after going about for alms, repair to the outskirts of the wood, let him go and sit down near the root of a tree.

'Applying himself to meditation, and being wise, let him find his pleasure in the outskirts of the wood, let him meditate at the root of a tree enjoying himself.

'Then when night is passing away, let him repair to the outskirts of the village, let him not delight in being invited nor in what is brought away from the village.

'Let not the Muni, after going to the village, walk about to the houses in haste; cutting off all talk while seeking food, let him not utter any coherent speech.

'"What I have obtained that is good," "I did not get anything that is good," so thinking in both cases he returns to the tree unchanged.

'Wandering about with his alms-bowl in his hand, considered dumb without being dumb let him not disregard a little gift, let him not despise the giver.

'Various are the practices illustrated by the Samana, they do not go twice to the other shore, this is not once thought.

'For whom there is no desire, for the Bhikkhu who has cut off the stream of existence and abandoned all kinds of work, there is no pain.'

'I wIll declare to thee the state of wisdom,'— so said Bhagavat,—'let one be like the edge of a razor, having struck his palate with his tongue, let him be restrained in regard to his stomach.

'Let his mind be free from attachment, let him not think much about worldly affairs, let him be without defilement, independent, and devoted to a religious life.

'For the sake of a solitary life and for the sake of the service that is to be carried out by Samanas, let him learn, solitariness is called wisdom; alone indeed he will find pleasure.

'Then he will shine through the ten regions, having heard the voice of the wise, of the meditating, of those that have abandoned sensual pleasures, let my adherent then still more devote himself to modesty and belief.

'Understand this from the waters in chasms and chasms and cracks: noisy go the small waters, silent goes the vast ocean.

'What is deficient that makes a noise, what is full that is calm; the fool is like a half-filled waterpot, the wise is like a full pool.

'When the Samana speaks much that is possessed of good sense, he teaches the Dhamma while, knowing it, while knowing it he speaks much.

'But he who while knowing it is self-restrained, and while knowing it does not speak much, such a Muni deserves wisdom, such a Muni has attained to wisdom.'

12.

The Many Reasons of Pain

(Dvayatanupassana Sutta)

All pain in the world arises from Upadhi, Avijja, Samkhara, Vinnana, Phassa, Vedana, Tanha, Arambha, Ahara, Injita, Nissaya, Rupa, Mosadhamma, Sukha.

So it was heard by me:

At one time Bhagavat dwelt at Savatthi in Pubbarama, Migaramatar's mansion. At that time Bhagavat on the Uposatha day on the fifteenth, it being full moon, in the evening was sitting in the open air, surrounded by the assembly of Bhikkhus. Then Bhagavat surveying the silent assembly of Bhikkhus addressed them as follows:

'Whichever Dhammas there are, O Bhikkhus, good, noble, liberating, leading to perfect enlightenment,—what is the use to you of listening to these good, noble, liberating Dhammas, leading to perfect enlightenment? If, O Bhikkhus, there should be people that ask so, they shall be answered thus: 'Yes, for the right understanding of the two Dhammas.' 'Which two do you mean?' 'I mean, "this is pain, this is the origin of pain," this is one consideration, "this is the destruction of pain, this is the way leading to the destruction of pain," this is the second consideration; thus, O Bhikkhus, by the Bhikkhu that considers the Dyad duly, is strenuous, ardent, resolute, of two fruits one fruit is to be expected: in this world perfect knowledge, or if any of the five attributes still remain the state of an Anagamin one that does not return.' This said Bhagavat, and when Sugata had said this, the Master further spoke:

'Those who do not understand pain and the origin of pain, and where pain wholly and totally is stopped, and do not know the way that leads to the cessation of pain,

'They, deprived of the emancipation of thought and the emancipation of knowledge, are unable to put an end to Samsara, they will verily continue to undergo birth and decay.

'And those who understand pain and the origin of pain, and where pain wholly and totally is stopped, and who know the way that leads to the cessation of pain,

'They, endowed with the emancipation of thought and the emancipation of knowledge, are able to put an end to Samsara they will not undergo birth and decay.

' "Should there be a perfect consideration of the Dyad in another way," if, O Bhikkhus, there are people that ask so, they shall be told, there is, and how there is: "Whatever pain arises is all in consequence of the **Upadhis**, elements of existence" this is one consideration, "but from the complete destruction of the Upadhis through absence of passion, there is no origin of pain," this is the second considieration; thus, O Bhikkhus, by the Bhikkhu that considers the Dyad duly, that is strenuous, ardent, resolute, of two fruits one fruit is to be expected: in this world perfect knowledge, or, if any of the five attributes still remain, the state of an Anagamin, one that does not return; this said Bhagavat, and when Sugata had said this, the Master further spoke:

'Whatever pains there are in the world, of many kinds, they arise having their cause in the Upadhi; that that fool again undergoes pain; therefore being wise do not create Upadhi, considering what is the birth and origin of pain.

Lord Buddha at Bagan, Myanmar

' "Should there be a perfect consideration of the Dyad in another way," if, O Bhikkhus, there are people that ask so, they shall be told, there is, and how there is: "Whatever pain arises is all in consequence of **Avijja**, ignorance," this is one consideration, "but from the complete destruction of Avijja, through absence of passion, there is no origin of pain," this is the second consideration; thus, O Bhikkhus, by the Bhikkhu that considers the Dyad duly, that is strenuous, ardent, resolute, of two fruits one fruit is to be expected: in this world perfect knowledge, or, if any of the five attributes still remain, the state of an Anagamin, one that does not return.' This said Bhagavat, and when Sugata had said this, the Master further spoke:

'Those who again and again go to Samsara with birth and death, to existence in this way or in that way, —that is the state of Avijja.

'For this Avijja is the great folly by which this existence has been traversed long, but those beings who resort to knowledge do not go to rebirth.

' " Should there be a perfect consideration of the Dyad in another way," if, O Bhikkhus, there are people that ask so, they shall be told, there is and how there is: "Whatever pain arises is all in consequence of the **Samkharas**, matter," this is one consideration, "but from the complete destruction of the Samkharas, through absence of passion, there is no origin of pain," this is the second consideration; thus, O Bhikkhus, by the Bhikkhu that considers the Dyad duly, that is strenuous, ardent, resolute, of two fruits one fruit is to be expected: in this world perfect knowledge, or, if any of the five attributes still remain, the state of an Anagamin, one that does not return.' This said Bhagavat, and when Sugata had said this, the Master further spoke:

'Whatever pain arises is all in consequence of the Samkharas, by the destruction of the Samkharas there will be no origin of pain.

'Looking upon this pain that springs from the Samkharas as misery, from the cessation of all the

Samkharas, and from the destruction of consciousness will arise the destruction of pain, having understood this exactly,

'The wise who have true views and are accomplished, having understood all things completely, and having conquered all association with Mara, do not go to rebirth.

' "Should there be a perfect consideration of the Dyad in another way," if, O Bhikkhus, there are people that ask so, they shall be told, there is and how there is: "Whatever pain arises is all in consequence of **Vinnana,** consciousness," this is one consideration, "but from the complete destruction of Vinnana, through absence of passion, there is no origin of pain," this is the second consideration; thus, O Bhikkhus, by the Bhikkhu that considers the Dyad duly. that is strenuous, ardent, resolute, of two fruits one fruit is to be expected: in this world perfect knowledge, or, if any of the five attributes still remain, the state of an Anagamin, one that does not return.' This said Bhagavat, and when Sugata had said this, the Master further spoke:

'Whatever pain arises is all in consequence of Vinnana, by the destruction of Vinnana there is no origin of pain.

'Looking upon this pain that springs from Vinnana as misery, from the cessation of Vinnana is Bhikkhu free from desire will be perfectly happy.'

' " Should there be a perfect consideration of the Dyad in another way," if, O Bhikkhus, there are people that ask so, they shall be told, there is, and how there is: "Whatever pain arises is all in consequence of **Phassa**, touch," this is one consideration, "but from the complete destruction of Phassa, through absence of passion, there is no origin of pain," this is the second consideration; thus, O Bhikkhus, by the Bhikkhu that considers the Dyad duly, that is strenuous, ardent, resolute, of two fruits one fruit is to be expected: in this world perfect knowledge, or, if any of the five attributes still remain, the state of an Anagamin, one that does not return.' This said Bhagavat, and when Sugata had said this, the Master further spoke:

'For those who are ruined by Phassa, who follow the stream of existence, who have entered a bad way, the destruction of bonds is far off.

'But those who, having fully understood Phassa, knowingly have taken delight in cessation, they verily from the destruction of Phassa and being free from desire, are perfectly happy.'

' "Should there be a perfect consideration of the Dyad in another way," if, O Bhikkhus, there are people that ask so, they shall be told, there is, and how there is: "Whatever pain arises is all in consequence of the **Vedanas,** sensations," this is one consideration, "but from the complete destruction of the Vedanas, through absence of passion, there is no origin of pain," this is the second consideration; thus, O Bhikkhus, by the Bhikkhu that considers the Dyad duly, that is strenuous, ardent, resolute, of two fruits one fruit is to be expected: in this world perfect knowledge, or, if any of the five attributes still remain, the state of an Anagamin, one that does not return.' This said Bhagavat, and when Sugata had said this, the Master further spoke:

'Pleasure or pain, together with want of pleasure and want of pain, whatever is perceived internally and externally,

'Looking upon this as pain, having touched what is perishable and fragile, seeing the decay of everything, the Bhikkhu is disgusted, having from the perishing of the Vedanas become free from desire and perfectly happy.'

'"Should there be a perfect consideration of the Dyad in another way," if, O Bhikkhus, there are people that ask so, they shall be told, there is, and how there is: "Whatever pain arises is all in consequence of **Tanha**, craving," this is one consideration, "but from the complete destruction of Tanha, through absence of passion, there is no origin of pain," this is the second consideration; thus, O Bhikkhus, by the Bhikkhu that considers the Dyad duly, that is strenuous, ardent, resolute, of two fruits one fruit is to be expected: in this world perfect knowledge, or, if any of the five attributes still remain, the state of an Anagamin, one that does not return.' This said Bhagavat, and when Sugata had said this, the Master further spoke:

'A man accompanied by Tanha, for a long time transmigrating into existence in this way or that way, does not overcome transmigration, Samsara.

'Looking upon this as misery, this origin of the pain of Tanha, let the Bhikkhu free from Tanha, not seizing upon anything, thoughtful, wander about.'

' "Should there be a perfect consideration of the Dyad in another way," if, O Bhikkhus, there are people that ask so, they shall be told, there is, and how there is: "Whatever pain arises is all in consequence of the **Upadanas**, the seizures;" this is one consideration, "but from the complete destruction of the Upadanas, through absence of passion there is no origin of pain," this is the second consideration; thus, O Bhikkhus, by the Bhikkhu that considers the Dyad duly, that is strenuous, ardent, resolute, of two fruit one fruit is to be expected: in this world perfect knowledge, or, if any of the five attributes still remain, the state of Anagamin, one that does not return.' This said Bhagavat, and when Sugata had said this, the Master further spoke:

'The existence is in consequence of the Upadanas; he who has come into existence goes to pain, he who has been born is to die, this is the origin of pain.

'Therefore, from the destruction of the Upadanas the wise with perfect knowledge, having seen what causes the destruction of birth, do not go to rebirth.'

'"Should there be a perfect consideration of the Dyad in another way," if, O Bhikkhus, there are people that ask so, they shall be told, there is and how there is: "Whatever pain arises is all in consequence of the **Arambhas,** exertions," this is one consideration, "but from the complete destruction of the Arambhas, through absence of passion.' there is no origin of pain," this is the second consideration, thus O Bhikkhus, by the Bhikkhu that considers the Dyad duly, that is strenuous, ardent, resolute, of two fruits one fruit is to be expected in this world: perfect knowledge, or, if any of the five attributes still remain, the state of an Anagamin, one that does not return.' This said Bhagavat, and when Sugata had said this, the Master further spoke:

'Whatever pain arises is all in consequence of the Arambhas, by the destruction of the Arambhas there is no origin of pain.

'Looking upon this pain that springs from the Arambhas as misery, having abandoned all the Arambhas, birth and transmigration have been crossed over by the Bhikkhu who is liberated in non-exertion, who has cut off the craving for existence, and whose mind is calm; there is for him no rebirth.'

' "Should there be a perfect consideration of the Dyad in another way," if, O Bhikkhus, there are people that ask so, they shall be told, there is, and how there is: "Whatever pain arises is all in consequence of the **Aharas**, food," this is one consideration, " but from the complete destruction of the Aharas, through absence of passion, there is no origin of pain," this is the second consideration; thus, O Bhikkhus, by the Bhikkhu that considers the Dyad duly, that is strenuous, ardent, resolute, of two fruits one fruit is to be expected: in this world perfect knowledge, or, if any of the five attributes still remain, the state of an Anagamin, one that does not return.' This said Bhagavat and when Sugata had said this, the Master further spoke:

'Whatever pain arises is all in consequence of the Aharas, by the destruction of the Aharas there is no origin of pain.

Anand, Lord Buddha's Disciple, Cave 26

'Looking upon this pain that springs from the Aharas as misery, having seen the result of all Aharas, not resorting to all Aharas.

'Having seen that health is from the destruction of desire, he that serves discriminatingly and stands fast in the Dhamma cannot be reckoned, existing, being accomplished.'

' "Should there be a perfect consideration of the Dyad in another way," if, O Bhikkhus, there are people that ask so, they shall be told, there is, and how there is: "Whatever pain arises is all in consequence of the **Injitas**, commotions," this is one consideration, "but from the complete destruction of the Injitas, through absence of passion, there is no origin of pain," this is the second consideration; thus, O Bhikkhus, by the Bhikkhu that considers the Dyad duly, that is strenuous, ardent, resolute, of two fruits one fruit is to be expected: in this world perfect knowledge, or, if any of the five attributes still remain, the state of an Anagamin, one that does not return.' This said Bhagavat and when Sugata had said this, the Master further spoke:

'Whatever pain arises is all in consequence of the Injitas, by the destruction of the Injitas there is no origin of pain.

'Looking upon this pain that springs from the Injitas as misery, and therefore having abandoned the Injitas and having stopped the Samkharas, let the Bhikkhu free from desire and not seizing upon anything, thoughtful, wander about.'

' "Should there be a perfect consideration of the Dyad in another way," if, O Bhikkhus, there are people that ask so, they shall be told, there is, and how there is: "For the **Nissita**, dependent, there is vacillation," this is one consideration, "the independent man does not vacillate," this is the second consideration; thus, O Bhikkhus, by the Bhikkhu that considers the Dyad duly, that is strenuous, ardent, resolute, of two fruits one fruit is to be expected: in this world perfect knowledge, or, if any of the five attributes still remain, the state of an Anagamin, one that does not return.' This said Bhagavat, and when Sugata had said this, the Master further spoke:

'The independent man does not vacillate, and the dependent man seizing upon existence in one way or in another, does not overcome Samsara.

'Looking upon this as misery and seeing great danger in things you depend upon, let a Bhikkhu wander about independent, not seizing upon anything, thoughtful.'

' "Should there be a perfect consideration of the Dyad in another way," if, O Bhikkhus, there are people that ask so, they shall be told, there is, and how there is: "The formless beings, O Bhikkhus, are calmer than the **Rupas**, form-possessing," this is one consideration, "cessation is calmer than the formless," this is another consideration; thus, O Bhikkhus, by the Bhikkhu that considers the Dyad duly, that is strenuous, ardent, resolute, of two fruits one fruit is to be expected: in this world perfect knowledge, or, if any of the five attributes still remain, the state of an Anagamin, one that does not return.' This said Bhagavat, and when Sugata had said this, the master further spoke:

'Those beings who are possessed of form, and those who dwell in the formless world, not knowing cessation, have to go to rebirth.

'But those who, having fully comprehended the forms, stand fast in the formless worlds, those who are liberated in the cessation, such beings leave death behind.'

' "Should there be a perfect consideration of the Dyad in another way," if, O Bhikkhus, there are people that ask so, they shall be told, there is and how there is: "What has been considered true by the world of men, together with the gods, Mara, Brahmin, and amongst the Samanas, Brahmins, gods, and men, that has by the noble through their perfect knowledge been well seen to be really false," this is one consideration; "what, O Bhikkhus, has been considered false by the world of men, together with the gods, Mara, Brahmin, and amongst the Samanas, Brahmins, gods, and men, that has by the noble through their perfect knowledge been well seen to be really true," this is another consideration. Thus, O Bhikkhus, by the Bhikkhu that considers the Dyad duly, that is strenuous, ardent, resolute, of two fruits one fruit is to be expected: in this world perfect knowledge, or, if any of the five attributes still remain, the state of an Anagamin, one that does not return.' This said Bhagavat, and when Sugata had said this, the Master further spoke:

'Seeing the real in the unreal, the world of men and gods dwelling in name and form, he thinks: "This is true."

'Whichever way they think it, it becomes otherwise, for it is perishable to him, and what is perishable is wretched.

'What is not perishable, the Nibbana, that the noble conceive as true, they verily from the comprehension of truth are free from desire; and perfectly happy.'

' "Should there be a perfect consideration of the Dyad in another way, if, O Bhikkhus, there are people that ask so, they shall be told, there is, and how there is: "What, O Bhikkhus, has been considered pleasure by the world of men, gods, Mara, Brahmin, and amongst the Samanas, Brahmins, gods, and men, that has by the noble by their perfect knowledge been well seen to be really pain," this is one consideration; "what, O Bhikkhus, has been considered pain by the world of men, gods, Mara, Brahmin, and amongst the Samanas, Brahmins, gods, and men, that has by the noble by their perfect knowledge been well seen to be really pleasure," this is the second consideration, Thus, O Bhikkhus, by the Bhikkhu who considers the Dyad duly, who is strenuous, ardent, resolute, of two fruits one fruit is to be expected: in this world perfect knowledge, or, if any of the five attributes still remain, the state of an Anagamin, one who does not return; This said Bhagavat, and when Sugata had said so, the Master further dpoke:

'Form, sound, taste, smell, and touch are all wished for, pleasing and charming things as long as they last, so it is said.

'By you, by the world of men and gods these things are deemed a pleasure, but when they cease it is deemed pain by them.

'By the noble the cessation of the existing body is regarded as pleasure; this is the opposite of what the wise in all the world hold.

'What fools say is pleasure that the noble say is pain, what fools say is pain that the noble know as pleasure:— see here is a thing difficult to understand, here the ignorant are confounded.

'For those that are enveloped there is gloom, for those that do not see there is darkness, and for the good it is manifest, for those that see there is light; even being near, those that are ignorant of the way and the Dhamma, do not discern anything,

'By those that are overcome by the passions of existence, by those that follow the stream of existence, by those that have entered the realm of Mara, this Dhamma is not perfectly understood.

'Who except the noble deserve the well understood state of Nibbana? Having perfectly conceived this state, those free from passion are completely extinguished.'

This spoke Bhagavat. Glad those Bhikkhus rejoiced at the words of Bhagavat. While this explanation was being given, the minds of sixty Bhikkhus, not seizing upon anything, were liberated.

❖❖❖

Cave 9

The Meanings Section

(Atthakavagga)

1.
AVOID SENSUAL PLEASURES LIKE SNAKE
(KAMA SUTTA)

Sensual pleasures are to be avoided.

If he who desires sensual pleasures is successful, he certainly becomes glad-minded, having obtained what a mortal wishes for.

But if those sensual pleasures fail the person who desires and wishes for them he will suffer, pierced by the arrow of pain:

He who avoids sensual pleasures as he would avoid treading upon the head of a snake with his foot, such a one, being thoughtful, will conquer this desire.

He who covets extensively such pleasures as the fields, goods, or gold, cows and horses, servants, women, relations,

Sins will overpower him, dangers will crush him, and pain will follow him as waste pours into a broken ship.

Therefore, let one always be thoughtful, and avoid pleasures; having abandoned them, let him cross the stream, after baling out the ship, and go to the other shore.

2.

Those Trembling in Selfishness

(Guhatthaka Sutta)

Let no one cling to existence and sensual pleasures.

A man that lives adhering to the cave, the body, who is covered with much sin, and sunk into delusion, such a one is far from seclusion, for the sensual pleasures in the world are not easy to abandon.

Those whose wishes are their motives, those who are linked to the pleasures of the world, they are difficult to liberate, or they cannot be liberated by others, looking for what is after or what is before, coveting these and former sensual pleasures.

Those who are greedy of, given to, and infatuated by sensual pleasures, those who are niggardly, they, having entered upon what is wicked, wail when they are subjected to pain, saying: 'What will become of us when we die, away from here?'

Therefore, let a man here learn, whatever he knows as wicked in the world, let him not for the sake of that practise what is wicked; for short is this life, say the wise.

I see in the world this trembling race given to desire for existences; they are wretched men who lament in the mouth of death, not being free from the craving for reiterated existences.

Look upon those men trembling in selfishness, like fish in a stream nearly dried up, with little water; seeing this, let one wander about unselfish without forming any attachment to existences.

Having subdued his wish for both ends, having fuily understood touch without being greedy, not doing what he has himself blamed, the wise man does not cling to what is seen and heard.

Having understood name, let the Muni cross over the stream, not defiled by any grasping; having pulled out the arrow of passion, wandering about strenuous, he does not wish for this world or the other.

3.
No Philosophies Will Help
(Dutthatthaka Sutta)

The Muni undergoes no censure, for he has shaken off all systems of philosophy, and is therefore independent.

Verily, some wicked-minded people censure. and also just-minded people censure, but the Muni does not undergo the censure that has arisen; therefore, there is not a discontented Muni anywhere.

How can he who is led by his wishes and possessed by his inclinations overcome his own false view? Doing his own doings let him talk according to his understanding.

The person who, without being asked, praises his own virtue and holy works to others, him the good call ignoble, one who praises himself.

But the Bhikkhu who is calm and of a happy mind, 'so I am,' thus not praising himself for his virtues, him the good call noble, one for whom there are no desires anywhere in the world.

He whose Dhammas are arbitrarily formed and fabricated, placed in front, and, because he sees in himself a good result, is therefore given to the view which is called *Kuppa-patichchasanti.*

For the dogmas of philosophy are not easy to overcome, amongst the Dhammas now this and now that is adopted after consideration; therefore a man rejects and adopts now this and now that Dhamma amongst the dogmas.

For him who has shaken off sin there is nowhere in the world any prejudiced view of the different existences; he who has shaken off sin, after leaving deceit and arrogance behind, which way should he go, he is independent.

But he who is dependent undergoes censure amongst the Dhammas; with what name and how should one name him who is independent? For by him there is nothing grasped or rejected, he has in this world shaken off every philosophical view.

4.

Behave Not like A Monkey

(Suddhatthaka Sutta)

No one is purified by philosophy, those devoted to philosophy run from one teacher to another, but the wise are not led by passion, and do not embrace anything in the world as the highest.

I see a pure, most excellent, sound man, by his views a man's purification takes place, holding this opinion, and having seen this view to be the highest, he goes back to knowledge, thinking to see what is pure.

If a man's purification takes place by his philosophical views, or he by knowledge leaves pain behind, then he is purified by another way than the Ariyamagga, the noble way, together with his Upadhis on account of his views he tells him to say so.

But the Brahmin who does not cling to what has been seen, or heard, to virtue and holy works, or to what has been thought, to what is good and to what is evil, and who leaves behind what has been grasped, without doing anything in this world, he does not acknowledge that purification comes from another.

Having left their former teacher they go to another, following their desires they do not break asunder their ties; they grasp, they let go like a monkey letting go one branch to catch hold of another.

Having himself undertaken some holy works he goes to various things led by his senses, but a man of great understanding, a wise man who by his wisdom has understood the Dhamma, does not go to various occupations.

Lord Buddha, Thailand

He being secluded amongst all the Dhammas, whatever has been seen, heard, or thought—how should anyone in this world be able to alter him, the seeing one, who wanders openly?

They do not form any view, they do not prefer anything, they do not say, 'I am infinitely pure;' having cut the tied knot of attachment they do not long for anything anywhere in the world.

He is a Brahmin that has conquered sin; by him there is nothing embraced after knowing and seeing it; he is not affected by any kind of passion; there is nothing grasped by him as the highest in this world.

5.

No Resting-Places for the Mind

(Paramatthaka Sutta)

One should not give oneself to philosophical disputations; a Brahmin who does not adopt any system of philosophy, is unchangeable, has reached Nibbana.

What one person, abiding by the philosophical views, saying, 'This is the most excellent, considers the highest in the world, everything different from that he says is wretched, therefore he has not overcome dispute.

Because he sees in himself a good result with regard to what has been seen or heard, virtue and holy works, or what has been thought, therefore having embraced that, he looks upon everything else as bad.

The expert call just that a tie dependent upon which one looks upon anything else as bad. Therefore, let a Bhikkhu not depend upon what is seen, heard, or thought, or upon virtue and holy works.

Let him not form any philosophical view in this world, either by knowledge or by virtue and holy works, let him not represent himself equal to others, nor think himself either low or distinguihshed.

Having left what has been grasped, not seizing upon anything he does not depend even on knowledge. He does not associate with those that are taken up by different things, he does not return to any philosophical view.

For whom there is here no desire, for both ends, for reiterated existence either here or in another world, for him there are no resting-places of the mind embraced after investigation amongst the doctrines.

In him there is not the least prejudiced idea with regard to what has been seen, heard, or thought; how could anyone in this world alter such a Brahmin who does not adopt any view?

They do not form any view, they do not prefer anything, the Dhammas are not chosen by them, a Brahmin is not dependent upon virtue and holy work; having gone to the other shore, such a one does not return.

6.

Neither Pleased Nor Displeased

(Jara Sutta)

From selfishness come grief and avarice. The Bhikkhu who has turned away from the world and wanders about houseless, is independent, and does not wish for purification through another.

Short indeed is this life, within a hundred years one dies, and if anyone lives longer, then he dies of old age.

People grieve from selfishness, perpetual cares kill them, this world is full of disappointment; seeing this, let one not live in a house.

That even of which a man thinks 'this is mine' is left behind by death: knowing this, let not the wise man turn himself to worldliness while being my follower.

As a man awakened does not see what he has met with in his sleep, so also he does not see the beloved person that has passed away and is dead.

Both seen and heard are the persons whose particular name is mentioned, but only the name remains undecayed of the person that has passed away.

The greedy in their selfishness do not leave sorrow, lamentation, and avarice; therefore, the Munis leaving greediness wandered about seeing security, Nibbana.

For a Bhikkhu, who wanders about unattached and cultivates the mind of a recluse, they say it is proper that he does not show himself agian in existence.

Under all circumstances the independent Muni does not please nor displease any one; sorrow and avarice do not stick to him as little as water to a leaf.

As a drop of water does not stick to a lotus, as water does not stick to a lotus, so a Muni does not cling to anything, namely, to what is seen or heard or thought.

He who has shaken off sin does not therefore think much of anything because it has been seen or heard or thought; he does not wish for purification through another, for he is not pleased nor displeased with anythingt.

7.

Firmly Keep to Your Solitary Life

(Tissametteyya Sutta)

Sexual intercourse should be avoided.

'Tell me, 0 venerable one,'—so said the venerable Tissa Metteyya,—'the defeat of him who is given to sexual intercourse; hearing thy precepts we will learn in seclusion.'

'The precepts of him who is given to sexual intercourse, 0 Metteyya,'—so said Bhagavat,—'are lost, and he employs himself wrongly, this is what is ignoble in him.

'He who, having formerly wandered alone, gives himself up to sexual intercourse, him they call in the world a low, common fellow, like a rolling chariot.

'What honour and renown he had before, that is lost for him; having seen this let him learn to give up sexual intercourse.

'He who overcome by his thoughts meditates like a miser, such a one, having heard the blaming voice of others, becomes discontented.

'Then he makes weapons, commits evil deeds urged by the doctrines of others, he is very greedy, and sinks into falsehood.

'Designated "wise" he has entered upon a solitary life, then having given himself up to sexual intercourse, he being a fool suffers pain.

'Looking upon this as misery let the Muni from first to last in the world firmly keep to his solitary life, let him not give himself up to sexual intercourse.

'Let him learn seclusion, this is the highest for noble men, but let him not therefore think himself the best, although he is verily near Nibbana.

'The Muni who wanders void of desire, not coveting sensual pleasures, and who has crossed the stream, him the creatures that are tied in sensual pleasures envy.'

8.

Branding Each Other as Fools

(Pasura Sutta)

Disputants brand each other as fools, they wish for praise, but being repulsed they become discontented; one is not purified by dispute, but by keeping to Buddha, who has shaken off all sin.

Here they maintain 'purity', in other doctrines they do not allow purity, what they have devoted themselves to, that they call good, and they enter extensively upon the single truths.

Those wishing for dispute, having plunged into the assembly, brand each other as fools mutually, they go to others and pick a quarrel, wishing for praise and calling themselves the only expert.

Engaged in dispute in the middle of the assembly, wishing for praise he lays about on all sides; but when his dispute has been repulsed he becomes discontented, at the blame he gets angry, he who sought for the faults of others.

Because those who have tested his questions say that his dispute is lost and repulsed, he laments and grieves having lost his disputes; 'he has conquered me,' so saying he wails.

These disputes have arisen amongst the Samanas, in these disputes there is dealt blow and stroke; having seen this, let him leave off disputing, for there is no other advantage to obtain from getting praise.

Or he is praised there, having cleared up the dispute in the middle of the assembly; therefore, he will laugh and be elated, having won that case as he had a mind to.

That which is his exaltation will also be the field of his defeat, still he talks proudly and arrogantly; seeing this, let no one dispute, for the experts do not say that purification takes place by that.

As a hero nourished by kingly food goes about roaring, wishing for an adversary—where he, the philosopher, Ditthigatika, is, go thou there, O hero; formerly there was nothing like this to fight against.

Those who, having embraced a certain philosophical view, dispute and maintain 'this only is true,' to them say thou when a dispute has arisen, 'here is no opponent for thee.'

Those who wander about after having secluded themselves, without opposing view to view—what opposition wilt thou meet with amongst those, O Pasura, by whom nothing in this world is grasped as the best?

Then thou wentest to reflection thinking in thy mind over the different philosophical views; thou hast gone into the yoke with him who has shaken off all sin, but thou wilt not be able to proceed together with him.

9.

'Buddha, Have My Daughter'

(Magandiya Sutta)

A dialogue between Magandiya and Buddha. The former offers Buddha his daughter for a wife, but Buddha refuses her. Magandiya says that purity comes from philosophy, Buddha 'from inward peace': The Muni is a confessor of peace, he does not dispute, he is free from marks.

A Dance Pose, Java

Buddha: 'Even seeing Tanha, Arati, and Raga, the daughters of Mara, there was not the least wish in me for sexual intercourse. What is this thy daughter's body but a thing full of water and excrement? I do not even want to touch it with my foot.'

Magandiya: 'If thou dost not want such a pearl, a woman desired by many kings, what view, virtue, and holy works, mode on life, rebirth dost thou profess?'

"'This I say," so I do now declare, after investigation there is nothing amongst the doctrines which such a one as I would embrace, Magandiya,'—so said Bhgavat,—and seeing misery in the philosophical views, without adopting any of them, searching for truth I saw "inward peace."

'All the philosophical resolutions that have been formed,'—so said Magandiya,—'those indeed thou explainest without adopting any of them; the notion "inward peace" which thou mention, how is this explained by the wise?'

'Not by any philosophical opinion, not by tradition, not by knowledge, Magandiya,'—so said Bhagavat,—not by virtue and holy works can any one say that purity exists; not by absence of philosophical opinion, by absence of tradition, by absence of knowledge, by absence of virtue and holy works either; having abandoned these without adopting anything else' let him, calm and independent, not desire existence.'

'If one cannot say by any philosophical opinion, or by tradition, or by knowledge,'—so said Magandiya,—'or by virtue and holy works that purity exists, nor by absence of philosophical opinion, by absence of tradition, by absence of knowledge, by absence of virtue and holy works, then consider the doctrine foolish, for by philosophical opinions some return to purity.'

'And asking on account of thy philosophical opinion, O Magandiya,'—so said Bhagavat,—'thou hast gone to infatuation in what thou hast embraced and of this inward peace thou hast not the least idea, therefore thou holdest it foolish.

'He who thinks himself equal to others or distinguished, or low, he for that very reason disputes; but he who is unmoved under those three conditions, for him the notion "equal" and "distinguished" do not exist.

'The Brahmin for whom the notion "equal" and "unequal" do not exist, would he say, "This is true?" Or with whom should he dispute, saying, "This is false?" With whom should he enter into dispute?

'Having left his house, wandering about houseless, not making acquaintances in the village, free from lust, not desiring any future existence, let the Muni not get into quarrelsome talk with people.

'Let not an eminent man dispute after having embraced those views separated from which he formerly wandered in the world; as the thorny lotus Elambuja is undefiled by water and mud, so the Muni, the confessor of peace, free from greed, does not cling to sensual pleasures and the world.

'An accomplished man does not by a philosophical view, or by thinking become arrogant, for he is not of that sort; not by holy works, nor by tradition is he to be led, he is not led into any of the resting places of the mind.

'For him who is free from marks there are no ties, to him who is delivered by understanding there are no follies; but those who grasped after marks and philosophical views, they wander about in the world annoying people.'

10.

A Calm Muni Is He

(Purabheda Sutta)

Definition of a calm muni.

'With what view and with what virtue is one called calm, tell me that, O Gotama, when asked about the best man?'

'He whose craving is departed before the dissolution of his body,'—so said Bhagavat,—'who does not depend upon beginning and end, nor reckons upon the middle, by him there is nothing preferred.

'He who is free from anger, free from trembling, free from boasting, free from misbehaviour, he who speaks wisely, he who is not elated, he is indeed a Muni who has restrained his speech.

'Without desire for the future he does not grieve for the past, he sees seclusion in the Phasses, touch, and he is not led by philosophical views.

'He is unattached, not deceitful, not covetous, not envious, not impudent, not contemptuous, and not given to slander.

'Without desire for pleasant things and not given to conceit and being gentle intelligent, not credulous, he is not displeased with anything

Not from love of gain does he learn and he does not get angry on account of loss, and untroubled by craving he has no greed for sweet things.

'Equable, always thoughtful, he does not think himself equal to others in the world, nor distinguished, nor low: for him there are no desires.

'The man in whom there is nothing upon which he depends, who is independent, having understood the Dhamma, in whom there is no craving for coming into existence or leaving existence,

'Him I call calm, not looking for sensual pleasures; for him there are no ties, he has overcome desire.

'For him there are no sons, cattle, fields, wealth, nothing grasped or rejected is to be found in him.

'That fault of which common people and Samanas and Brahmins say that he is possessed, is not possessed by him, therefore he is not moved by their talk.

'Free from covetousness, without avarice, the Muni does not reckon himself amongst the distinguished, nor amongst the plain, nor amongst the low, he does not enter time, being delivered from time.

'He for whom there is nothing in the world which he may call his own, who does not grieve over what is no more, and does not walk the Dhammas after his wish, he is called calm.'

11.
Ceasing to Exist
(Kalahavivada Sutta)

The origin of contentions, disputes, etc.

'Whence do spring up contentions and disputes, lamentation and sorrow together with envy; and arrogance and conceit together with slander, whence do these spring up? pray, tell me this.'

'From dear objects spring up contentions and disputes, lamentation and sorrow together with envy; arrogance and conceit together with slander; contentions and disputes are joined with envy, and there is slander in the disputes arisen.'

'The dear objects in the world whence do they originate, and whence the covetousness that prevails in the world, and desire and fulfilment whence do they originate, which are, of consequence for the future state of a man?'

'From wish originate the dear objects in the world, and the covetousness that prevails in the world, and desire and fulfilment originate from it, which are of consequence for the future state of a man.'

'From what has wish in the world its origin, and resolutions whence do they spring, anger and falsehood and doubt, and the Dhammas which are made known by Samana Gotama?'

'What they call pleasure and displeasure in the world, by that wish springs up; having seen decay and origin in all bodies a person forms his resolutions in the world.

'Anger and falsehood and doubt, these Dhammas are a couple; let the doubtful learn in the way of knowledge, knowingly the Dhammas have been proclaimed by the Samana.'

'Pleasure and displeasure, whence have they their origin, for want of what do these not arise? This notion which thou mention, "decay and origin," tell me from what does this arise.'

'Pleasure and displeasure have their origin from Phassas, touch, when there is no touch they do not arise. This notion which thou mention, "decay and origin," this I tell thee has its origin from this.'

'From what has Phassa its origin in the world, and from what does grasping spring up? For want of what is there no egotism, by the cessation of what do the touches not touch?'

'On account of name and form the touches exist, grasping has its origin in wish; by the cessation of wishes there is no egotism, by the cessation of form the touches do not touch.'

'How is one to be constituted that his form may cease to exist, and how do joy and pain cease to exist? Tell me this, how it ceases, that we should like to know, such was my mind?'

'Let one not be with a natural consciousness, nor with a mad consciousness, nor without consciousness, nor with his consciousness gone; for him who is thus constituted form ceases to exist, for what is called delusion has its origin in consciousness.'

'What we have asked thee thou hast explained unto us; we will ask thee another question, answer us that; Do not some, who are considered wise in this world tell us that the principal thing is the purification of the Yakkha, or do they say something different from this?'

'Thus some who are considered wise in this world say that the principal thing is the purification of the Yakkha; but some of them say Samaya, annihilation, the expert say that the highest purity lies in Anupadisesa, none of the five attributes remaining.

Lord Buddha, Java

'And having known these to be dependent, the investigating Muni, having known the things we depend upon, and after knowing them being liberated, does not enter into dispute, the wise man does not go to reiterated existence.'

12.

Dogmatist No Leader to Purity

(Chulaviyuha Sutta)

A description of disputing philosophers. The different schools of philosophy contradict each other, they proclaim different truths, but the truth is only one. As long as the disputations are going on, so long will there be strife in the world.

Abiding by their own views, some people, having got into contest, assert themselves to be the only expert, saying, who understands this he knows the Dhamma, he who reviles this he is not perfect.

So having got into contest they dispute: 'The opponent is a fool, an ignorant person, so they say. Which one of these, pray, is the true doctrine? For all these assert themselves to be the only expert.

He who does not acknowledge an opponent's doctrine, he is a fool, a beast, one of poor understanding, all are fools with a very poor understanding; all these abide by their own views.

They are surely purified by their own views, they are of a pure understanding, expert, thoughtful, amongst them there is no one of poor understanding, their views are quite perfect.

I do not say, 'This is the reality,' which fools say mutually to each other; they made their own views the truth, therefore they hold others to be fools.

What some say is the truth, the reality, that others say is void, false, so having disagreed they dispute. Why do not the Samanas say one and the same thing?

For the truth is one, there is not a second, about which one intelligent man might dispute with another intelligent man; but they themselves proclaim different truths, therefore, the Samanas do not say one and the same thing.

Why do the disputants that assert themselves to be the only expert, proclaim different truths? Have many different truths been heard of, or do they only follow their own reasoning?

There are not many different truths in the world, no eternal ones except consciousness; but have reasoned on the philosophical views they proclaim a double Dhamma, truth and falsehood.

In regard to what has been sccn, or heard, virtue and holy works, or what has been thought, and on account of these views, looking upon others with contempt, standing in their resolutions joyful, they say that the opponent is a fool and an ignorant person.

Because he holds another to be a fool, therefore he calls himself expert, in his own opinion he is one that tells what is propitious, others he blames, so he said.

He is full of his overbearing philosophical view, mad with pride, thinking himself perfect, he is in his own opinion anointed with the spirt of genius, for his philosophical view is quite complete.

If he according to another's report is low, then he says the other is also of a low understanding, and if he himself is accomplished and wise, there is not any fool amongst the Samanas.

'Those who preach a doctrine different from this, fall short of purity and are imperfect,' so the Titthiyas say repeatedly, for they are inflamed by passion for their own philosophical views.

Here they maintain purity, in other doctrines they do not allow purity; so the Titthiyas, entering extensively upon details, say that in their own way there is something firm.

And saying that there is something firm in his own way he holds his opponent to be a fool; thus he himself brings on strife, calling his opponent a fool and impure.

Standing in his resolution, having himself measured teachers, etc., he still more enters into dispute in the world; but having left all resolutions nobody will excite strife in the world.

13.

Be Indifferent to Learning

(Mahaviyuha Sutta)

Philosophers cannot lead to purity, they only praise themselves and stigmatise others. But a Brahmin has overcome all dispute, he is indifferent to learning, he is appeased.

Those who abiding in the philosophical views dispute, saying, 'This is the truth,' they all incur blame, and they also obtain praise in this matter.

This is little, not enough to bring about tranquillity, I say there are two fruits of dispute; having seen this let no one dispute, understanding Khema, Nibbana, to be the place where there is no dispute.

The opinions that have arisen amongst people, all these the wise man does not embrace; he is independent. Should he who is not pleased with what has been seen and heard resort to dependency.

Those who consider virtue the highest of all, say that purity is associated with restraint; having taken upon themselves a holy work they serve. Let us learn in this view, then, his, the Master's, purity; wishing for existence they assert themselves to be the only expert.

If he falls off from virtue and holy works, he trembles, having missed his work; he taments, prays for purity in this world, as one who has lost his caravan or wandered away from his house.

Having left virtue and holy works altogether, and both wrong and blameless work, not praying for purity or

Looking into a Mirror, Cave 17

impurity, he wanders abstaining from both purity and impurity, without having embraced peace.

By means of penance, or anything disliked, or what has been seen, or heard, or thought, going upwards they wail for what is pure, without being free from craving for reiterated existence.

For him who wishes for something there always are desires, and trembling in the midst of his plans; he for whom there is no death and no rebirth, how can he tremble or desire anything?

What some call the highest Dhamma, that others again call wretched; which one of these, pray, is the true doctrine? for all these assert themselves to be the only expert.

Their own Dhamma they say is perfect, another's Dhamma again they say is wretched; so having disagreed they dispute, they each say their own opinions are the truth.

If one becomes low by another's censure, then there will be no one distinguished amongst the Dhammas; for they all say another's Dhamma is low, in their own they say there is something firm.

The worshipping of their own Dhamma is as great as their praise of their own ways; all schools would be in the same case, for their purity is individual.

There is nothing about a Brahmin dependent upon others, nothing amongst the Dhammas which he would embrace after investigation; therefore, he has overcome the disputes, for he does not regard any other Dhamma as the best.

'I understand, I see likewise this,' so saying, some by their philosophical views return to purity. If he saw purity, what then has been effected by another's view? Having conquered they say that purity exists by another.

A seeing man will see name and form, and having seen he will understand those things; let him at pleasure see much or little, for the expert do not say that purity exists by that.

A dogmatist is no leader to purity, being guided by prejudiced views, saying that good consists in what he is given to, and saying that purity is there, he saw the thing so.

A Brahmin does not enter time, or the number of living beings, he is no follower of philosophical views, nor a friend of knowledge; and having penetrated the opinions that have arisen amongst people, he is indifferent to learning, while others acquire it.

The Muni, having done away with ties here in the world, is no partisan in the disputes that have arisen; appeased amongst the unappeased he is indifferent, not embracing learning, while others acquire it.

Having abandoned his former passions, not contracting new ones, not wandering according to his wishes, being no dogmatist, he is delivered from the philosophical views, being wise, and he does not cling to the world neither does he blame himself.

Being secluded amongst all the doctrines, whatever has been seen, heard, or thought, he is a Muni who has laid down his burden and is liberated, not belonging to time, not dead, not wishing for anything. So said Bhagavat.

14.

The Inwardly Appeased

(Tuvataka Sutta)

How a Bhikkhu attains bliss, what his duties are, and what he is to avoid.

'I ask thee, who art a kinsman of the Adichchas and a great Isi, about seclusion and the state of peace. How is a Bhikkhu, after having seen it, extinguished, not grasping at anything in the world?'

'Let him completely cut off the root of what is called delusion, thinking "I am wisdom;" so said Bhagavat,—'all the cravings that arise inwardly, let him learn to subdue them, always being thoughtful.

'Let him learn every Dhamma inwardly or outwardly; let him not therefore be proud, for that is not called bliss by the good.

'Let him not therefore think himself better than others or low or equal to others; questioned by different people, let him not adorn himself.

'Let the Bhikkhu be appeased inwardly, let him not seek peace from any other quarter, for him who is inwardly appeased there is nothing grasped or rejected.

'As in the middle of the sea no wave is born but as it remains still, so let the Bhikkhu be still, without desire, let him not desire anything whatever.'

He with open eyes expounded clearly the Dhamma that removes all dangers; tell now the religious practices; the precepts or contemplation.

Bhagavat: 'Let him not be greedy with his eyes, let him keep his ears from the talk of the town, let him not be greedy after sweet things, and let him not desire anything in the world.

'When he is touched by the touch of illness, let the Bhikkhu not lament, and let him not wish for existence anywhere, and let him not tremble at dangers.

'Having obtained boiled rice and drink, solid food and clothes, let him not store up these things and let him not be anxious, if he does not get them.

'Let him be meditative, not prying, let him abstain from misbehaviour, let him not be indolent, let the Bhikkhu live in his quiet dwelling.

'Let him not sleep too much, let him apply himself ardently to watching, let him abandon sloth, deceit, laughter, sport, sexual intercourse, and adornment.

'Let him not apply himself to practising the hymns of the Athabbanaveda, to the interpretation of sleep and signs: nor to astrology; let not my follower devote himself

Lord Buddha, Polannaruva

to interpreting the cry of birds, to causing impregnation, nor to the art of medicine.

'Let the Bhikkhu not tremble at blame, nor puff himself up when praised; let him drive off covetousness together with avarice, anger, and slander.

'Let the Bhikkhu not be engaged in purchase and sale, let him not blame others in anything, let him not scold in the village, let him not from love of gain speak to people.

'Let not the Bhikkhu be a boaster, and let him not speak coherent language; let him not learn pride, let him not speak quarrelsome language.

'Let him not be led into falsehood, let him not consciously do wicked things; and with respect to livelihood, understanding, virtue, and holy works, let him not despise others.

'Having heard much talk from much-talking Samanas, let him not irritated answer them with harsh language; for the good do not thwart others.

'Having understood this Dhamma, let the investigating and always thoughtful Bhikkhu learn; having conceived bliss to consist in peace, let him not be indolent in Gotama's commandments.

'For he a conqueror unconquered saw the Dhamma visibly, without any traditional instruction; therefore let him learn, heedful in his, Bhagavat's commandments, and always worshipping.'

15.

A Muni Is He . . .

(Attadanda Sutta)

Description of an accomplished Muni.

From a stick seized fear arises. Look at people killing each other; I will tell of grief as it is known to me.

Seeing people struggling like fish in a pond with little water, seeing them obstructed by each other, a fear came over me.

The world is completely unsubstantial, all quarters are shaken; wishing for a house for myself I did not see one uninhabited.

But having seen all being in the end obstructed, discontent arose in me; then I saw in this world an arrow, difficult to see, stuck in the heart.

He who has been pierced by this arrow runs through all quarters; but having drawn out that arrow, he will not run, he will sit down quietly.

There many studies are gone through; what is tied in the world let him not apply himself to untie it; having wholly transfixed desire, let him learn his own extinction, Nibbana.

Let the Muni be truthful, without arrogance, undeceitful, free from slander, not angry, let him overcome avarice.

Let the man who has turned his mind to Nibbana conquer sleepiness, drowsiness, and sloth; let him not live together with indolence, let him not indulge in conceit.

Let him not be led into falsehood, let him not turn his affection to form; let him penetrate arrogance, let him wander abstaining from violence.

Let him not delight in what is old, let him not bear with what is new, let him not grieve for what is lost, let him not give himself up to desire.

This desire I call greed, the great stream, I call it precipitation, craving, a trouble, a bog of lust difficult to cross.

The Muni who without deviating from truth stands fast on the firm ground of Nibbana, being a Brahmin, he, having forsaken everything, is indeed called calm.

He indeed is wise, he is accomplished, having understood the Dhamma independent of everything; wandering rightly in the world he does not envy anyone here.

Whosoever has here overcome lust, a tie difficult to do away with in the world, he does not grieve, he does not covet, having cut off the stream, and being without bonds.

What is before thee, lay that aside; let there be nothing behind thee; if thou wilt not grasp after what is in the middle, thou wilt wander calm.

The man who has no desire at all for name and form, individuality, and who does not grieve over what is no more, he indeed does not decay in the world.

He who does not think, 'this is mine' and 'for others there is also something,' he, not having egotism, does not grieve at having nothing.

Not being harsh, not greedy, being without desire, and being the same under all circumstances,—that I call a good result, when asked about an undaunted man.

For him who is free from desire, for the discerning man there is no Samkhara; abstaining from every sort of effort he sees happiness everywhere.

The Muni does not reckon himself amongst the plain, nor amongst the low, nor amongst the distinguished; being calm and free from avarice, he does not grasp after nor reject anything.

16.

Let Him Overcome

(Sariputta Sutta)

On Sariputta asking what a Bhikkhu is to devote himself to, Buddha shows what life he is to lead.

'Neither has before been seen by me,'—so said the venerable Sariputta,—'nor has anyone heard of such a beautifully-speaking master, a teacher arrived from the Tusita heaven.

Cave 1

'As he, the clearly-seeing, appears to the world of men and gods, after having dispelled all darkness, so he wanders alone in the midst of people.

'To this Buddha, who is independent, unchanged, a guileless teacher, who has arrived in the world, I have come supplicatingly with a question from many who are bound in this world.

'To a Bhikkhu who is loath of the world and affects an isolated seat, the root of a tree or a cemetery, or who lives in the caves of the mountains,

'How many dangers are there not in these various dwelling-places at which the Bhikkhu does not tremble in his quiet dwelling.

'How many dangers are there not in the world for him who goes to the immortal region, dangers which the Bhikkhu overcomes in his distant dwelling.

'Which are his words, which are his objects in this world, which are the virtue and holy works of the energetic Bhikkhu?'

'What study having devoted himself to, intent on one object, wise and thoughtful, can he blow off his own filth as the smith blows off that of the silver,

'What is pleasant for him who is disgusted with birth etc., O Sariputta,'—so said Bhagavat,—'if he cultivates a lonely dwelling-place, and loves perfect enlightenment in accordance with the Dhamma, that I will tell thee as I understand it.

'Let not the wise and thoughtful Bhikkhu wandering on the borders be afraid of the five dangers: gadflies and all other flies, snakes contact with evil men, and quadrupeds.

'Let him not be afraid of adversaries, even having seen many dangers from them; further he will overcome other dangers while seeking what is good.

'Touched by sickness and hunger let him endure cold and excessive heat, let him, touched by them in many ways, and being houseless, make strong exertions.

'Let him not commit theft, let him not speak falsely, let him touch friendly what is feeble or strong, what he acknowledges to be the agitation of the mind, let him drive that off as a partisan of Kanha, i.e., Mara.

'Let him not fall into the power of anger and arrogance; having dug up the root of these, let him live, and let him overcome both what is pleasant and what is unpleasant.

'Guided by wisdom, taking delight in what is good, let him scatter those dangers, let him overcome discontent in his distant dwelling, let him overcome the four causes of lamentation.

'What shall I eat, or where shall I eat?—he lay indeed uncomfortably last night—where shall I lie this night? let the Sekha who wanders about houseless subdue these lamentable doubts.

'Having had in due time both food and clothes, let him know moderation in this world for the sake of happiness; guarded in these things and wandering restrained in the village, let him, even if he be irritated, not speak harsh words.

'Let him be with downcast eyes, and not prying, devoted to meditation, very watchful; having acquired equanimity, let him with a composed mind cut off the seat of doubt, and misbehaviour.

'Urged on by words of his teachers, let him be thoughtful and rejoice at this urging, let him break stubbornness in his fellow-students, let him utter propitious words and not unseasonable, let him not think detractingly of others.

'And then the five impurities in the world, the subjection of which he must learn thoughtfully,—let him overcome passion for form, sound and taste, smell and touch.

'Let the Bhikkhu subdue his wish for these Dhammas and be thoughtful, and with his mind well liberated, then in time he will, reflecting upon Dhamma, and having become intent upon one object. destroy darkness.' So said Bhagavat.

❖❖❖

Cave 6

5

The Learning Section

(Parayana Vagga)

To the Brahmin Bavari, living on the banks of the Godavari, in Assaka territory, comes another Brahmin and asks for five hundred pieces of money, but not getting them he curses Bavari, saying, 'May thy head on the seventh day cleave into seven.' A deity comforts Bavari by referring him to Buddha. Then Bavari sends his sixteen disciples to Buddha, and each of them asks Buddha a question.

Bavari's Story

From the beautiful city of the Kosalas, Savatthi, a Brahmin, well versed in the hymns, went to the South Dakkhinapatha, wishing for nothingness.

In Assaka's territory, in the neighbourhood of Alaka, he dwelt on the banks of the Godavari, living on gleanings and fruit.

And close by the bank there was a large village, with the income of which he prepared a great sacrifice.

Having offered the great sacrifice, he again entered the hermitage. Upon his re-entering, another Brahmin arrived,

With swollen feet, trembling with dirty teeth, and with dust on his head. And he going up to him, the first Brahmin demanded five hundred pieces of money.

Bavari, seeing him, bade him to be seated, asked him whether he was happy and well, and spoke as follows:

'What gifts I had are all given away by me; pardon me, O Brahmin, I have no five hundred.'

'If thou wilt not give to me who asks, may thy head on the seventh day cleave into seven.'

So after the usual ceremonies this impostor made known his fearful curse. On hearing these his words Bavari became sorrowful.

He wasted away taking no food, transfixed by the arrow of grief, but yet his mind delighted in meditation.

Seeing Bavari struck with horror and sorrowful, the benevolent deity of that place approached him and said as follows:

'He does not know anything about the head; he is a hypocrite coveting riches; knowledge of the head and head-splitting is not found in him.'

'If the venerable deity knows it, then tell me, when asked, all about the head and head-splitting; let us hear thy words.'

'I do not know this; knowledge of it is not found in me; as to the head and head-splitting, this is to be seen by Buddhas only.'

'Who then, say, in the circumference of the earth knows the head and head-splitting, tell me that, O deity?'

'Formerly went out from Kapilavatthu a ruler of the world, an offspring of the king, the Sakya son, the light-giving;'

'He is, O Brahmin, the perfectly Enlightened Sambuddha; perfect in all things, he has attained the power of all knowledge, sees clearly in everything; he has arrived at the destruction of all things, and is liberated in the destruction of the Upadhis.

'He is Buddha, he is Bhagavat in the world, he, the clearly-seeing, teaches the Dhamma; go thou to him and ask, he will explain it to thee.'

Having heard the word 'Sambuddha,' Bavari rejoiced, his grief became little, and he was filled with great delight.

Bodhisattva

Bavari glad, rejoicing, and eager asked the deity: 'In what village or in what town or in what province dwells the chief of the world, that going there we may adore the perfectly Enlightened, the first of men?'

'In Savatthi, the town of the Kosalas, dwells Jina the Victorious, of great understanding and excellent wide knowledge, he the Sakya son, unyoked, free from passion, skilled in head-splitting, the bull of men.'

Then Bavari addressed his disciples, Brahmins, perfect in the hymns: 'Come, youths, I will tell you something, listen to my words:

'He whose appearance in the world is difficult to be met with often, he is at the present time born in the world and widely renowned as Sambuddha, the perfectly Enlightened; go quickly to Savatthi and behold the best of men.'

'How then can we know, on seeing him, that he is Buddha, O Brahmin? Tell us who do not know him, by what may we recognise him?'

'For in the hymns are to be found the marks of a great man, and thirty-two are disclosed altogether, one by one. 'For him on whose limbs these marks of a great man are to be found, there are two ways left, a third does not exist.

'If he abides in a dwelling, he will subdue this earth without rod or sword, he will rule with justice.

'And if he departs from his dwelling for the wilderness, he becomes the saint, incomparable Sambuddha, who has removed the veil from the world.

'Ask in your mind about my birth and family, my marks, hymns, and my other disciples, the head and head-splitting.

'If he is Buddha, the clear-sighted, then he will answer by word of mouth the questions you have asked in your mind.'

Having heard Bavari's words his disciples, sixteen Brahmins, Ajita, Tissametteyya, Punnaka, further Mettagu, Dhotaka and Upasiva, and Nanda, further Hemaka, the two Todeyya and Kappa, and the wise Jatukanni, Bhadravudha and Udaya, and also the Brahmin Posala, and the wise Mogharajan, and the great Isi Pingiya,

All of them, having each their host of pupils, and being themselves widely renowned throughout the world, thinkers delighting in meditation, wise, scented with the perfume of former good deeds.'

Having saluted Bavari and gone round him towards the right, all with matted hair and bearing hides, departed with their faces turned to the north.

To Patitthana of Alaka first, then to Mahissatt, and also to Ujjeni, Gonaddha, Vedisa, Vanasavhaya,

And also to Kosambi, Saketa, and Savatthi, the most excellent of cities, to Setavya, Kapilavatthu, and the city of Kusinara,

And to Pava, the city of wealth, to Vesali, the city of Magadha, to Pasanaka chetiya, the Rock Temple, the lovely, the charming.

As he who is athirst longs for the cold water, as the merchant longs for gain, as he who is plagued by heat longs for shade, so in haste they ascended the mountain.

And Bhagavat at that time attended by the assembly of the Bhikkhus taught the Dhamma to the Bhikkhus, and roared like a lion in the forest.

Ajita beheld Sambuddha as the shining sun without burning rays, as the moon on the fifteenth, having reached her plenitude.

'Then observing on his body all the marks in their fulness, standing apart, rejoiced, he asked the questions of his mind:

'Tell me about my master's birth, tell me about his family together with the marks, tell me about his perfection in the hymns, how many hymns does the Brahmin recite?'

Bhagavat said: 'One hundred and twenty years is his age, and by family he is a Bavari; three are his marks on the limbs, and in the three Vedas he is perfect.

'In the marks and in the Itihasa together with Nighandu and Ketubha—he recites five hundred—and in his own Dhamma he has reached perfection.'

Ajita thought: 'Explain fully the marks of Bavari, O thou best of men, who cuts off desire; let there be no doubt left for us.'

Bhagavat said: 'He covers his face with his tongue, he has a circle of hair between the eye-brows, his privy member is hidden in a sheath, know this, O young man.'

Not hearing him ask anything, but hearing the questions answered, the multitude reflected overjoyed and with joined hands.

'Who, be he a god, or Brahman, or Inda, the husband of Suja, asked in his mind those questions, and to whom did that speech reply?'

Ajita said: 'The head and head-splitting Bavari asked about; explain that, O Bhagavat, remove our doubt, O Isi.'

Bhagavat said: 'Ignorance is the head, know this; knowledge cleaves the head, together with belief, thoughtfulness, meditation, determination, and strength.'

Then with great joy having composed himself the young man put his hide on one shoulder, fell at Bhagavat's feet and saluted him with his head, saying:

'Bavari, the Brahmin, together with his disciples, O thou venerable man, delighted and glad, does homage to thy feet, O thou clearly-seeing.'

Bhagavat said: 'Let Bavari, the Brahmin, be glad together with his disciple! Be thou also glad, live long, O young man!

Lord Buddha, Borobudur

'For Bavari and for thee, for all there are all kinds of doubt; having got an opportunity, ask ye whatever you wish.'

After getting permission from Sambuddha, Ajita sitting there with folded hands asked Tathagata the first question.

AJITA'S QUESTION
(AJITAMANAVAPUCHCHHA)

'By what is the world shrouded,'—so said the venerable Ajita,—'by what does it not shine? What callest thou its pollution, what is its great danger?'

'With ignorance is the world shrouded, O Ajita,'—so said Bhagavat,—'by reason of avarice it does not shine; desire I call its pollution, pain is its great danger.'

'The streams of desire flow in every direction,'—so said the venerable Ajita;—' what dams the streams, say what restrains the streams, by what may the streams be shut off?'

'Whatever streams there are in the world, O Ajita,'—so said Bhagavat,—'thoughtfulness is their dam, thoughtfulness I call the restraint of the streams, by understanding they are shut off.'

'Both understanding and thoughtfulness,'—so said the venerable Ajita,—'and name and shape, O venerable man, —asked about this by me, declare by what is this stopped?'

Buddha: 'This question which thou hast asked, O Ajita, that I will explain to thee; I will explain to thee by what name and shape are totally stopped; by the cessation of consciousness this is stopped here.'

Ajita: 'Those who have examined any Dhammas, i.e., the saints, and those who are disciples, and those who are common men here,—when thou art asked about their mode of life, declare it unto me, thou who are wise, O venerable man.'

Buddha: 'Let the Bhikkhu not crave for sensual pleasures, let him be calm in mind, let him wander about skilful in all Dhammas, and thoughtful.'

Tissa's Question

(Tissametteyyamanavapuchchha)

'Who is contented in the world,' —so said the venerable Tissametteyya,—'who is without commotions? Who after knowing both ends does not stick in the middle, as far as his understanding is concerned? Whom dost thou call a great man? Who has overcome desire in this world?'

'The Bhikkhu who abstains from sensual pleasures, O Metteyya,'—so said Bhagavat,—'who is free from desire, always thoughtful, happy by reflection, he is without commotions, he after knowing both ends does not stick in the middle, as far as his understanding is concerned; him I call a great man, he has overcome craving in this world.'

Punnaka's Question

(Punnkamanavapuchchha)

'To him who is without desire, who has seen the root of sin,'—so said the venerable Punnaka,—'I have come supplicatingly with a question: On account of what did the Isis and men, Khattiyas and Brahmins, offer sacrifices to the gods abundantly in this world? about this I ask thee, O Bhagavat, tell me this.'

'All these Isis and men, Khattiyas and Brahmins, O Punnaka,' —so said Bhagavat,—'who offered sacrifices to the gods abundantly in this world, offered sacrifices, O Punnaka, after reaching old age, wishing for their present condition.'

'All these Isis and men, Khattiyas and Brahmins,'—so said the venerable Punnaka,—'who offered sacrifices to the gods abundantly in this world, did they, O Bhagavat, indefatigable in the way of offering, cross over both birth and old age, O venerable man? I ask thee, O Bhagavat, tell me this.'

'They wished for, praised, desired, abandoned sensual pleasures, O Punnaka,'—so said Bhagavat,—'they desired sensual pleasures on account of what they reached by them; they, devoted to offering, dyed with the passions of existence, did not cross over birth and old age, so I say.'

'If they, devoted to offering,'—so said the venerable Punnaka,—'did not by offering cross over birth and old age, O venerable man, who then in the world of gods and men crossed over birth and old age, O venerable man, I ask this thee, O Bhagavat, tell me this?'

'Having considered everything in the world, O Punnaka,'—so said Bhagavat,—'he for whom there is no commotion anywhere in the world, who is calm without the smoke of passions, free from woe, free from craving, he crossed over birth and old age, so I say.'

Mettagu's Question
(Mettagumanavapuchchha)

'I ask thee, O Bhagavat, tell me this,'—so said the venerable Mettagu,—'I consider thee accomplished and of a cultivated mind, why are these creatures, whatsoever they are of many kinds in the world, always subject to pain?'

'Thou mayest well ask me concerning the origin of pain, O Mettagu,'—so said Bhagavat,—'I will explain that to thee in the way I myself know it: originating in the Upadhis pains arise, whatsoever they are, of many kinds in the world.

'He who being ignorant creates Upadhi, that fool again undergoes pain; therefore, let not the wise man create Upadhi considering that this is the birth and origin of pain.'

Mettagu: 'What we have asked thee thou hast explained to us; another question I ask thee, answer that, pray: How

Bodhisattva Padmapani

do the wise cross the stream, birth and old age, and sorrow and lamentation? Explain that thoroughly to me, O Muni, for this thing, Dhamma, is well known to thee.'

'I will explain the Dhamma to thee, O Mettagu,'— so said Bhagavat; —'if a man in the visible world, without any traditional instruction, has understood it, and wanders about thoughtful, he may overcome desire in the world.'

Mettagtu: 'And I take delight in that, in the most excellent Dhamma, O great Isi, which if a man has understood, and he wanders about thoughtful, he may overcome desire in the world.'

'Whatsoever thou knowest, O Mettagu—so said Bhagavat,—'of what is above, below, across, and in the middle, taking no delight and no rest in these things, let thy mind not dwell on existence.

'Living so, thoughtful, strenuous, let the Bhikkhu wandering about, after abandoning selfishness, birth, and old age, and sorrow, and lamentation, being a wise man, leave pain in this world.'

Mettagu: 'I delight in these words of the great Isi; well expounded, O Gotama, is by thee freedom from Upadhi, i.e., Nibbana. Bhagavat in truth has left pain, for this Dhamma is well known to thee.

'And those also will certainly leave pain whom thou, O Muni, constantly mayest admonish; therefore I bow down to thee, having come hither, O chief, may Bhagavat also admonish me constantly.'

Buddha: 'The Brahmin whom I may acknowledge as accomplished, possessing nothing, not cleaving to the world of lust, he surely has crossed this stream, and he has crossed over to the other shore, free from harshness, and free from doubt.

'And he is a wise and accomplished man in this world; having abandoned this cleaving to reiterated existence he is without craving, free from woe, free from longing, he has crossed over birth and old age, so I say.'

Dhotaka's Question

(Dhotakamanavapuchchha)

'I ask thee, O Bhagavat, tell me this,'—so said the venerable Dhotaka,—'I long for thy word, O great Isi; may one, having listened to thy utterance, learn his own extinction.'

Lord Buddha, Srilanka

'Exert thyself then, O Dhotaka,'—so said Bhagavat,—'being wise and thoughtful in this world let one, having listened to my utterance, learn his own extinction.'

Dhotaka: 'I see in the world of gods and men a Brahmin wandering about, possessing nothing; therefore I bow down to thee, O thou all seeing one, free me, O Sakka, from doubts.'

Buddha: 'I shall not go to free anyone in the world who is doubtful, O Dhotaka; when thou hast learned the best Dhamma, then thou shalt cross this stream.'

Dhotaka: 'Teach me, O Brahmin, having compassion on me the Dhamma of seclusion, i.e., Nibbana, that I may understand it and that, without falling into many shapes like the air, may wander calm and independent in this world.'

'I will explain to thee peace, O Dhotaka,'—so said Bhagavat—'if a man in the visible world, without any traditional instruction, has understood it, and wanders about thoughtful, he may overcome desire in the world.'

Dhotaka: 'And I take delight in that, the highest peace, O great Isi, which if a man has understood, and he wanders about thoughtful, he may overcome desire in the world.'

'Whatsoever thou knowest, O Dhotaka,'—so said Bhagavat, —'of what is above, below, across, and in the middle, knowing this to be a tie in the world, thou must not thirst for reiterated existence.'

Upasiva's Question

(Upasivamanavapuchchha)

'Alone, O Sakka, and without assistance I shall not be able to cross the great stream,' —so said the venerable Upasiva;—'tell me an object, O thou all-seeing one, by means of which one may cross this stream.'

'Having in view nothingness, being thoughtful, O Upasiva,' —so said Bhagavat,—'by the reflection of nothing existing shalt thou cross the stream; having abandoned sensual pleasures, being loath of doubts, thou shalt regard the extinction of craving, i.e.,Nibbana, both day and night.'

Upasiva: 'He whose passion for all sensual pleasures has departed, having resorted to nothingness, after leaving everything else, and being delivered in the highest deliverance by knowledge, will he remain there without proceeding further?'

'He whose passion for all sensual pleasures has departed, O Upasiva,'—so said Bhagavat,—'having resorted to nothingness after leaving everything else, and being delivered in the highest deliverance by knowledge, he will remain there without proceeding further.'

Upasiva: 'If he remains there without proceeding further for a multitude of years, O thou all-seeing one, and if he becomes there tranquil and delivered, will there be consciousness for such a one?'

"As a flame blown about by the violence of the wind, O Upasiva,'—so said Bhagavat,—'goes out, cannot be reckoned as existing; even so a Muni, delivered from name and body, disappears, and cannot be reckoned as existing.'

Upasiva: 'Has he only disappeared, or does he not exist any longer, or is he for ever free from sickness? Explain that thoroughly to me, O Muni, for this Dhamma is well known to thee.'

'For him who has disappeared there is no form, O Upasiva,'—so said Bhagavat,—'that by which they say he is, exists for him no longer, when all things, Dhamma, have been cut off, all kinds of dispute are also cut off.'

NANDA'S QUESTION

(NANDAMANAVAPUCHCHHA)

'There are Munis in the world,'—so said the venerable Nanda,—'so people say. How is this understood by thee? Do they call him a Muni who is possessed of knowledge or him who is possessed of life?'

Buddha: 'Not because of any philosophical view, nor of tradition, nor of knowledge, O Nanda, do the expert call any one a Muni; but such as wander free from woe, free from desire, after having secluded themselves, those I call Munis.'

'All these Samanas and Brahmins,'—so said the venerable Nanda,—'say that purity comes from philosophical views, and from tradition, and from virtue and holy works, and in many other ways. Did they, in the way in which they lived in the world, cross over birth and old age, O venerable man? I ask thee, O Bhagavat, tell me this.'

'All these Samanas and Brahmins, O Nanda,'—so said Bhagavat,—'say that purity comes from philosophical views, and from tradition, and from virtue and holy works, and in many other ways, still they did not, in the way in which they lived in the world, cross over birth and old age, so I say.'

'All these Samanas and Brahmins,'—so said the venerable Nanda,—'say that purity comes from philosophical views, and from tradition, and from virtue and holy works, and in many other ways; if thou, O Muni, sayest that such have not crossed the stream, who then in the world of gods and men crossed over birth and old age, O venerable man? I ask thee, O Bhagavat, tell me this.'

'I do not say that all Samanas and Brahmins, O Nanda,'—so said Bhagavat,—'are shrouded by birth and old age; those who, after leaving in this world what has been seen or heard or thought, and all virtue and holy works, after leaving everything of various kinds, after penetrating craving, are free from passion, such indeed I call men that have crossed the stream.'

Nanda: 'I delight in these words of the great Isi; well expounded by thee, O Gotama, is freedom from Upadhi, i.e., Nibbana; those who, after leaving in this world what has been seen or heard or thought, and all virtue and holy works, after leaving everything of various kinds, after penetrating craving, are free from passion, such I verily call men that have crossed the stream.'

Lord Buddha from Java

Hemaka's Question

(Hemakamanavapuchchha)

'Those who before,'—so said the venerable Hemaka, —'explained to me their doctrine, previously to Gotama's doctrine, saying, "So it was, so it will be," all that was only oral tradition, all that was only something that increased my doubts.

'I took no pleasure in that, but tell thou me the Dhamma that destroys craving, O Muni, which if a man has understood, and he wanders about thoughtful, he may cross desire in the world.'

Buddha: 'In this world much has been seen, heard, and thought; the destruction of passion and of wish for the dear objects that have been perceived, O Hemaka, is the imperishable state of Nibbana.

'Those who, having understood this, are thoughtful, calm, because they have seen the Dhamma, tranquil and divine, such have crossed desire in this world.'

Todeyya's Question

(Todeyyamanavapuchchha)

'He in whom there live no lusts,' —so said he venerable Todeyya,—'to whom there is no craving, and who has overcome doubt, what sort of deliverance is there for him?'

'He in whom there live no lusts, O Todeyya,'—so said Bhagavat,—'to whom there is no craving and who has overcome doubt, for him there is no other deliverance.'

Todeyya: 'Is he without desire or is he longing, is he possessed of understanding or is he forming himself an understanding? Explain this to me, O thou all-seeing one, that I may know a Muni, O Sakka.'

Buddha: 'He is without desire, he is not longing, he is possessed of understanding, and he is not forming himself an understanding; know, O Todeyya, that such is the

Cave 1

Muni, not possessing anything, not cleaving to lust and existence.'

Kappa's Question
(Kappamanavapuchchha)

'For those who stand in the middle of the water,'—so said the venerable Kappa,—'in the formidable stream that has set in, for those who are overcome by decay and death, tell me of an island, O venerable man, and tell thou me of an island that this pain may not again come on.'

'For those who stand in the middle of the water, O Kappa,'—so said Bhagavat,—'in the formidable stream that has set in, for those overcome by decay and death, I will tell thee of an island, O Kappa.

'This matchless island, possessing nothing and grasping after nothing, I call Nibbana, the destruction of decay and death.

'Those who, having understood this, are thoughtful and calm, because they have seen the Dhamma, do not fall into the power of Mara, and are not the companions of Mara.'

Jatukannin's Question
(Jatukannimanavapuchchha)

'Having heard of a hero free from lust,'—so said the venerable Jatukannin,—'who has crossed the stream, I have come to ask him who is free from lust; tell me the seat of peace, O thou with the born eye of wisdom, tell me this truly, O Bhagavat.

'For Bhagavat wanders about after having conquered lust as the hot sun conquers the earth by its heat; tell the Dhamma to me who has only little understanding, O thou of great understanding, that I may ascertain how to leave in this world of birth and decay.'

'Subdue thy greediness for sensual pleasures, Jatukannin,'—so said Bhagavat,—'having considered the

Stupa at Pagan

forsaking of the world as happiness, let there not be anything either grasped after or rejected by thee.

'What is before thee, lay that aside; let there be nothing behind thee; if thou wilt not grasp after what is in the middle, thou wilt wander calm.

'For him whose greediness for name and form is wholly gone, O Brahmin, for him there are no passions by which he might fall into the power of death.'

Bhadravudha's Question
(Bhadravudhamavavapuchchha)

'I entreat the wise Buddha, the houseless, who cuts off desire,'—so said the venerable Bhadravudha,—'who is free from commotion. forsakes joy, has crossed the stream, is liberated, and who leaves time behind; having heard the chief's word, they will go away from here.

'Different people have come together from the provinces, longing to hear thy speech, O hero; do thou expound it thoroughly to them, for this Dhamma is well known to thee.'

'Let one wholly subdue the craving of grasping after everything, O Bhadravudha,'—so said Bhagavat,—'above, below, across, and in the middle; for whatever they grasp after in the world, just by that Mara follows the man.

'Therefore, knowing this, let not the thoughtful Bhikkhu grasp after anything in all the world, considering as creatures of desire this generation, sticking fast in the realm of death.'

Udaya's Question
(Udayamanavapuchchha)

'To Buddha who is sitting meditating, free from pollution,'—so said the venerable Udaya,—'having performed his duty, who is without passion, accomplished in all things, Dhamma, I have come with a question; tell

Tara, Bagan

me the deliverance by knowledge, the splitting up of ignorance.'

'It consists in leaving lust and desire, O Udaya,'—so said Bhagavat,— 'and both kinds of grief, and driving away sloth, and warding off misbehaviour.

'The deliverance by knowledge which is purified by equanimity and thoughtfulness and preceded by reasoning on Dhamma I will tell thee, the splitting up of ignorance.'

Udaya: 'What is the bond of the world, what is its practice? By the leaving of what is Nibbana said to be?'

Buddha: 'The world is bound by pleasure, reasoning is its practice; by the leaving of desire Nibbana is said to be.'

Udaya: 'How does consciousness cease in him that wanders thoughtful? Having come to ask thee, let us hear thy words.'

Buddha: 'For him who both inwardly and outwardly does not delight in sensation, for him who thus wanders thoughtful, consciousness ceases.'

Posala's Question

(Posalamanavapuchchha)

'He who shows the past births, etc.,'—so said the venerable Posala,—'who is without desire and has cut off doubt, to him who is accomplished in all things, Dhamma, I have come supplicatingly with a question.

'O Sakka, I ask about his knowledge who is aware of past shapes, who casts off every corporeal form, and who sees that there exists nothing either internally or externailly, how can such a one be led by anybody?'

'Tathagata, knowing all the faces of consciousness, O Posala'—so said Bhagavat,—'knows also him who stands delivered, devoted to that object.

'Having understood that the bonds of pleasure do not originate in nothingness, he sees clearly in this matter, this is, the knowledge of a perfect, accomplished Brahmin.'

Mogharaja's Question

(Mogharajamanavapuchchha)

'Twice have I asked Sakka,'—so said the venerable Mogharaja,—'but the clearly-seeing has not explained it to me; if the divine Isi is asked for the third time, he will explain it, so I have heard.

'There is this world, the other world, Brahman's world together with the world of the gods; I do not know thy view, the famous Gotama's view.

'To this man who sees what is good I have come supplicatingly with a question: How is any one to look upon the world that the king of death may not see him?'

'Look upon the world as void, O Mogharajan, being always thoughtful; having destroyed the view of oneself as really existing, so one may overcome death; the king of death will not see him who thus regards the world.'

Pingiya's Question

(Pingiyamanavapuchchha)

'I am old, feeble, colourless,'—so said the venerable Pingiya,—'my eyes are not clear, my hearing is not good; lest I should perish a fool on the way, tell me the Dhamma, that I may know how to leave birth and decay in this world.'

'Seeing others afflicted by the body, O Pingiya,'—so said Bhagavat,—'seeing heedless people suffer in their bodies;—therefore, O Pingiya, shalt thou be heedful, and leave the body behind, that thou mayest never come to exist again.'

Pingiya: 'Four regions, four intermediate regions, above and below, these are the ten regions; there is nothing which has not been seen, heard, or thought by thee, and is there anything in the world not understood by thee?

Tell me the Dhamma, that I may know how to leave birth and decay in this world.'

'Seeing men seized with desire, O Pingiya,'—so said Bhagavat,—'tormented and overcome by decay,—therefore thou, O Pingiya, shalt be heedful, and leave desire behind, that thou mayest never come to exist again.'

●

This said Bhagavat, living in Magadha at Pasanaka Chetiya, the Rock Temple. Sought by sixteen Brahmins the followers of Bavari, and questioned by each of them in turn, he responded to the questions. If a man having understood the meaning and tenor of each question, lives according to the Dhamma, then he will go to the further shore of decay and death, for these Dhammas lead to the further shore, and therefore this order of Dhamma was called 'the way to the other shore.'

Ajita, Tissametteyya, Punnaka and Mettagu, Dhotaka and Upasiva, Nanda and Hemaka, the two Todeyya and Kappa, and the wise Jatukannin, Bhadravudha and Udaya, and also the Brahmin Posala, and the wise Mogharaja, and Pingiya the great Isi,

These went up to Buddha, the Isi of exemplary conduct; asking subtle questions they went up to the supreme Buddha.

Buddha, being asked, responded to their questions truly, and in responding to the questions the Muni delighted the Brahmins.

They, having been delighted by the clearly-seeing Buddha, the kinsman of the Adichchas, devoted themselves to a religious life near the man of excellent understanding.

He who lived according to what had been taught by Buddha in answer to each single question, went from this shore to the other shore.

From this shore he went to the other shore entering upon the most excellent way; this way is to lead to the

Ritual Bath, Cave 1

other shore, therefore it is called 'the way to the other shore.'

●

'I will proclaim accordingly the way to the further shore,'—so said the venerable Pingiya—'as he saw it, so he told it; the spotless, the very wise, the passionless, the desireless lord, for what reason should he speak falsely?

'Well! I will praise the beautiful voice of Buddha who is without stain and folly, and who has left behind arrogance and hypocrisy.

'The darkness-dispelling Buddha, the all-seeing, who thoroughly understands the world, has overcome all existences, is free from passion, has left behind all pain, is rightly called Buddha, he, O Brahmin, has come to me.

'As the bird, having left the bush, takes up his abode in the fruitful forest, even so I, having left men of narrow views, have reached the great sea, like the Hamsa.

'Those who before in another world explained the doctrine of Gotama, saying, "So it was, so it will be," all that was only oral tradition, all that was only something that increased my doubts.

'There is only one abiding dispelling darkness, that is the high-born, the luminous, Gotama of great understanding, Gotama of great wisdom,

'Who taught me the Dhamma, the instantaneous, the immediate, the destruction of desire, freedom from distress, whose likeness is nowhere.'

Bavari: 'Canst thou stay away from him even for a moment, O Pingiya, from Gotama of great understanding, from Gotama of great wisdom,

'Who taught thee the Dhamma, the instantaneous, the immediate, the destruction of desire, freedom from distress whose likeness is nowhere?'

Pingiya: 'I do not stay away from him even for a moment, O Brahmin, from Gotama of great understanding, from Gotama of great wisdom,

'Who taught me the Dhamma, the instantaneous, the immediate, the destruction of desire, freedom from distress, whose likeness is nowhere.

'I see him in my mind and with my eye, vigilant, O Brahmin, night and day; worshipping I spend the night, therefore I think I do not stay away from him.

'Belief and joy, mind and thought incline me towards the doctrine of Gotama; whichever way the very wise man goes, the very same I am inclined to.

'Therefore, as I am worn out and feeble, my body does not go there, but in my thoughts I always go there, for my mind, O Brahmin, is joined to him.

'Lying in the mud of lusts wriggling, I jumped from island to island; then saw the perfectly Enlightened, who has crossed the stream, and is free from passion.'

At the conclusion of this gatha, Bhagavat, who stayed at Savatthi, when seeing the maturity of the minds of Pingiya and Bavari, shed a golden light. Pingiya, who sat picturing Buddha's virtues to Bavari, having seen the light, looked round, saying, 'What is this?' And when he saw Bhagavat standing before him, he said to the Brahmin Bavari: 'Buddha has come.' The Brahmin rose from his seat and stood with folded hands. Bhagavat, shedding a light, showed himself to the Brahmin, and knowing what was beneficial for both, he said this stanza while addressing Pingiya:

'As Vakkali was delivered by faith, 'as well as Bhadravudha and Alavi-Gotama so thou shalt let faith deliver thee, and thou shalt go, O Pingiya, to the further shore of the realm of death!'

Pingiya: 'I am highly pleased at hearing the Muni's words; Sambuddha has removed the veil, he is free from harshness, and wise.

'Having penetrated all things concerning the gods, he knows everything of every description; the Master will put an end to all questions of the doubtful that will admit him.

'To the insuperable, the unchangeable Nibbana, whose likeness is nowhere, I shall certainly go; in this Nibbana there will be no doubt left for me, so know me to be of a dispossessed mind.'

❖❖❖

Buddham Sharnam

More Titles are Available in

PHILOSOPHY, RELIGION & CULTURE

1.	Kamasutra **(New)**	125/-
2.	The Kama Sutra of Mallinga Vatsyayana **(New)**	125/-
3.	The Golden Book of Hinduism **(New)**	250/-
4.	The Golden Book of Islam **(New)**	250/-
5.	The Life of Lord Buddha **(New)**	225/-
6.	The Discourses of Lord Buddha **(New)**	225/-
7.	My Experiment with Truth (PB) **(New)**	250/-
8.	Mahatma Gandhi's The Bhagavadgita (PB) **(New)**	125/-
9.	Vivekananda Select (PB) **(New)**	250/-
10.	Intellect India (PB) **(New)**	250/-
11.	Patriot: Netaji Subhas Chandra Bose **(New)**	250/-
12.	The Golden Book of Rigveda **(New)**	250/-
13.	The Golden Book of Jainism **(New)**	250/-
14.	The Golden Book of Upanishads **(New)**	250/-
15.	The Golden Book of Buddhism **(New)**	250/-
16.	Culture India **(New)**	250/-
17.	Shirdi Sai Baba **(New)**	80/-
18.	Learn Rajyoga from Vivekananda **(New)**	250/-

19. The Ramayana: For Every Home **(New)** 95/-

20. The Mahabharata: For Every Home **(New)** 125/-

21. Sai - The Age of Cosmic Family 75/-

22. Sathya Sai and His Miraculous Powers 95/-

23. To Bloom Like a Lotus 150/-

24. The History of Sikh Gurus 225/-

25. Intelligence Beyond Thought 295/-

26. Indian Mythology (PB) **(New)** 195/-

4263/3, Ansari Road,
Darya Ganj, New Delhi-110 002
Ph.: 32903912, 23280047,9811594448
E-mail: lotus_press@sify.com
www.lotuspress.co.in